Love Works

Love Works

That's the Gospel Truth

NED WISNEFSKE

WIPF & STOCK · Eugene, Oregon

LOVE WORKS
That's the Gospel Truth

Copyright © 2025 Ned Wisnefske. All rights reserved. Except for brief quotations in critical publications or reviews, no part of this book may be reproduced in any manner without prior written permission from the publisher. Write: Permissions, Wipf and Stock Publishers, 199 W. 8th Ave., Suite 3, Eugene, OR 97401.

Wipf & Stock
An Imprint of Wipf and Stock Publishers
199 W. 8th Ave., Suite 3
Eugene, OR 97401

www.wipfandstock.com

PAPERBACK ISBN: 979-8-3852-4635-9
HARDCOVER ISBN: 979-8-3852-4636-6
EBOOK ISBN: 979-8-3852-4637-3

06/12/25

The Scripture quotations contained herein are from the New Revised Standard Version Bible, copyright 1989, Division of Christian Education of the National Council of Churches of Christ in the United States of America. Used by permission. All rights reserved.

For Karen
Who made it work

Contents

Preface	ix
Introduction	1
Worldviews	3
What can we know? What ought we do? What might we hope?	9

PART ONE: WHAT CAN WE KNOW?

The world is headed for destruction. Why?	15
The world is headed for destruction. Why should we care?	26
What we can't know but might believe	40

PART TWO: WHAT OUGHT WE DO?

Pursue happiness	53
Preserve your life	57
Follow moral rules	62

PART THREE: WHAT MIGHT WE HOPE?

We are free	71
What might we hope for this world?	79
Leap to love	90
Love works	99
Bibliography	105
Index	109

Preface

The world is headed for destruction, in the long term and in the short term, on the universal scale and on the human. That is our best understanding of what is going on in the world. Why is this? Is it just because all matter is doomed to disintegrate? Is it God's plan to destroy the world? Those are two common responses. This essay will argue that it is not for either of those reasons, but because a pervasive disordering or chaos—a deep darkness, as the Bible puts it—works to put an end to the world, the universe as a whole, as well as human life. That's why the world is headed for destruction. That possibility is explored in *Could God Fail? The Fate of the Universe and the Faith of Christians*. This essay follows up that discussion.

It begins with the assumption that the destruction of the universe would be dreadful. Something is amiss when the future of our universe is to disintegrate into a formless void. Something is wrong with this picture: arising out of immense and unbounded energy, material takes form, and living things and even thinking beings emerge—only for everything to dissolve back into useless energy, into nothing. It looks, on the face of it, as though something went wrong, or was violated, or something promising was wasted. It should provoke dismay to see all the potential of the universe come to nothing, and we should be hard-pressed to explain what happened. If it does happen, how would we understand what is going on in the universe, where it came from, where it is going, and what our place is in it?

It would be lame to answer the question "What's going on in the universe?" in this way: things come into existence, connect and contend in various ways, then pass away until the universe itself ceases to exist. If that were all we could say, then the existence of human beings—emerging from unguided, random interactions of particles, who have not just brains but self-conscious minds, not just sensations but passions, not just instincts but free wills—would be incomprehensible. We need a better account, one that constructively explains where we came from, where we are going, and the purpose of human life. That human beings developed reason, affections, and free will, and used those capacities to love—to further the lives of others, even at the cost of their own lives—would leave us baffled. We should be astonished at this capacity because love acts contrary to strong impulses to look out for oneself—to defend one's own material, as it were—and we should want to account for this. How was it that the universe, consisting of material connecting and contending, and living things, struggling to gain an advantage over other living things, gave rise to beings who could empathize and love others, even though they might receive no material benefit in it, and even at their own expense?

Similarly, if we thought that God created the world from nothing and planned to consign it to nothing, what sense would it make to claim that God "loved the world" or that the world was "very good?" How such destruction was "love" would be incomprehensible; how this world was "very good" would be inscrutable. Was God displeased with the world? Will God try again? Is the creation a first step or prelude to another creation, or a trial run to see who earns entry into it? But then we would wonder: why would God create another world, unless this creation is not really so good after all, not really worthy of God's love? —And why would God become incarnate in—join the divine nature to—a nature that is doomed to come to nothing?[1]

The universe appears to exist under a death sentence. Is there any hope for it? Will anything prevent this future? Not if we believed that all matter in the universe is destined to disintegrate, or if we believed that God plans to destroy the universe. In either case, all our work to preserve the world will come to nothing, and all our efforts to oppose destructiveness are futile. This essay will argue that we should not be resigned to the disintegration of the universe or to the destruction of life on earth—and certainly we should not give up on humanity. We can have hope, rather, for the future of our world, and we should oppose the corruption and destructiveness that surround us. The basis for this hope is the belief that there is a purposeful plan and loving will that opposes the chaos threatening to destroy the universe.

This essay will argue that there is a better way to explain why we live in a universe that gave rise to intelligent beings capable of love and at the same time seems destined to disintegrate. Contrary to materialism, this was not a random occurrence. There are good reasons, we will see, to believe that there is a purposeful ordering that brought the world into being, sustains

---

1. John Polkinghorne takes a different view. He believes that a proper continuity between this age and the next is maintained with the concept creation *ex vetere*—that the new creation will be born out of the old—and with the idea that God's creative purpose is a "two-step process." The first creation explores its potentiality at some distance from God; the new creation is brought into the life of God. *Quest*, 106.

life, and can save the world from annihilation. At the same time, contrary to theism, there are good reasons to think that this purposefulness is not omniscient and omnipotent, but that it is contested and threatened by pervasive disordering. With an eye to the biblical point of view, we can believe that this purposefulness is intelligent, active in the world, and works to save the world. This belief, finally, gives us confidence that there is a future for this world in spite of the chaos looming around and ahead of us, and that we should live in that hope. We will refine these concepts and sharpen this context in the discussions that follow.

How, then, should we understand what is going on in the universe, where it came from, where it is going, and our place in it?

In brief, this essay will contend that the creation of our world was neither a random accident nor a first step, neither a matter of luck nor a prelude before its predestined destruction and replacement by heaven. Instead, we should see the creation of the universe as an act of deliverance. The initiative that brought the cosmos into being delivered it from a state of chaos.[2] From the biblical point of view, the creation of the universe, its evolution, and its promotion is a defiant act of love.

More fully: the beginning of the universe was an attack against a formless void, against the chaos that held its potential in bondage; the evolution of life was a challenge to lifelessness; and the development of self-consciousness was deliverance from darkness. From the biblical point of view, the reason there is a cosmos at all is because love defied primeval darkness: love freed a formless void from chaos so that matter could become a cosmos, so that living things could evolve and self-conscious beings develop—beings who themselves could care for the world and protect life from corruption and destruction. Because that is what is really going on in the universe, we are drawn to enter into that life-giving activity, to participate in it, and to continue it. Seeing that that is what is going on in the world, we

2. "Chaos," not in the technical physical sense where chaos can lead toward a higher level of order or operates unpredictably in an ordered universe, but as disruptive designs, discordant patterns, or disinformation that throws natural orderings into disorder. Bruce Lincoln explored the importance of chaos in several ancient myths. In his analysis, in the beginning was insubstantial stuff, rich in potential. Order and disorder came later. *Gods and Demons*, 117–19. These are several books challenging the idea that God's struggle with chaos lies behind Gen 1:1–2: Watson, *Chaos*; Tsumura, *Creation and Destruction*; Sollereder, *Evolution*. For a defense of the traditional understanding of creation *ex nihilo*, see Torrance, *Doctrine of God*, 207. It is not unusual to characterize the basic stuff of the universe as potentiality. We see this in both Western and Eastern thought. For Aristotle matter is primarily the bearer of potential. (Heisenberg applies this way of thinking to his understanding of subatomic particles. See *Philosophy*, 41.) The Dalai Lama discusses the importance of potentiality for Buddhist thought in *Universe*, 73–93.

are encouraged to choose paths that protect and promote life and to spurn those that undercut and corrupt it.[3]

And in general: the love of the Creator depicted in the Bible opposes all that enslaves—formless voids, futile existence, and all that holds bodies, minds, and wills in bondage—and works to free us from them. It is a defiant love because it faces real, formidable opposition—and so must be undaunted. It is costly and dear because it expends itself to free from such opposition. This biblical understanding of the love of God is of a love that works: it confronts opposition, strives against it, gives of itself in order to liberate from it, and succeeds. The creature, in turn, made in the likeness of the Creator, is commissioned to do the same.

That is the biblical worldview this essay puts forward. It is one that makes sense of what is going on in the world, of why we are here, of what we are to do with our lives, and of what we can hope for. It makes more sense than materialism, the view that all that exists is matter randomly coming together and coming apart, or theism, the view that an omnipotent and omniscient God created the world from nothing, miraculously intervenes in it, eventually destroys it, and then replaces it with heaven.

To develop this theological worldview, there are many objections to answer: "Why be concerned about the eventual destruction of the universe? That is simply the fate of all matter. Besides, the end is a long way off. So why not pursue happiness while we can?" Or, "If that happens, it must be God's will. Besides, we have heaven to look forward to." Or, "How can this be a biblical worldview? A biblical perspective is based on an omnipotent and omniscient God who miraculously intervenes in the world." And so forth. This essay intends to meet those objections. It aims to show that the theological worldview developed dignifies our humanity in a way that materialism cannot, and it inspires us to live up to our humanity in a way that theism does not. It does this by assuming the perspective of mortal, moral human beings—not immortal souls or amoral animals—who live in a world that appears to be doomed to destruction. The result is a worldview that enlivens us to live lives of faith, hope, and love—even if the world should disintegrate into nothingness.

---

3. Karl Barth presents a vigorous account of the reality and power of nothingness. But he even more forcefully claims that this negative aspect of creation nevertheless praises the Creator, so that any theology claiming that nothingness could triumph over creation is blasphemy. For Barth, the battle is over, the victory won. The task of theology is to proclaim that truth. *Dogmatics*, 3.3:352, 311, 303.

Introduction

The universe seems doomed to disintegrate. The universe came from a virtual nothingness and will return to nothingness. All living things and all intelligent beings that evolved from lifeless matter will return to lifelessness. This realization has to affect how we look at the universe and our place in it. It has to. If there is no future for the universe, what do we live for and what can we hope for? How should we live knowing that our efforts to make the world a better place will come to nothing? What is the purpose of life lived between eternities of lifelessness?

If the universe is to end in a cataclysmic explosion or turn into a formless void, as most cosmologists think, what would we conclude? We might conclude that the universe was a dud, a meaningless cosmic accident. In that case, cosmic pointlessness is the context for human life, which itself must be, ultimately, pointless. Or, from a theological point of view, we might conclude that it was the will of the Creator to destroy the universe—the Creator, then, being also the Destroyer. In that case, it is difficult to see why the Creator pronounced it "very good" or how "God loved the world." Why, then, should *we* care about its future and be good stewards of it? The point of our existence in this world, it would seem, could only be to gain existence in another world, in heaven, and to find as much happiness in this world as we can.

If we think that the universe is merely material—its creation a cosmic accident and its evolution and eventual destruction a series of random occurrences—then it has no purpose and there is no hope for our world. Or, if we think it is God's will to destroy the universe, then again it has no real purpose and there is no hope for it. This life could only be a preparation or training ground or first step for some future world; but again, *this* life has no ultimate meaning. In both cases, the final destruction of the universe would mean that all our efforts to improve our world are finally futile—pointless busyness. All we can do is labor for the happiness we can find in this life and perhaps strive for a life *after* this one. Either way, this world is ultimately purposeless.

Can we avoid these dismal conclusions? One way is to think that this universe isn't all there is (it really isn't a *universe*). It could be that this universe is part of a multiverse or an infinite number of universes. In that case, the end of this world really isn't the end at all; perhaps I will continue to exist in other worlds. Then I can believe that this life isn't all there is, and that other possibilities await me.[1] Why, then, be dismayed over the end of this world? There will be others, and I might live in them. Or, I could believe I am going to heaven. In that case, the end of the world doesn't really matter to me either. Earth will be destroyed, it will be replaced with heaven, and I will live there forever. So why be concerned about the fate of Earth, or of the universe, for that matter? Foreseeing the destruction of life on Earth could even be a comfort because it signals the coming of heaven.

From the perspective of this essay, these ways of reconciling ourselves to the destruction of the universe are only wishful thinking or wistful dreaming. Any "hope" we had would be nothing more than wishful thinking—crossing fingers for luck in this world and for a future existence in some other world. Or, if I were religious, "hope" would amount to praying for happiness in this world and dreaming about a future existence in heaven. Such "hope" could not evoke convictions to preserve, protect, and promote life on Earth. With no hope that our world has a future, moreover, our responsibility for life on Earth, not to mention any concern to leave this world better than we found it, would dissolve. From either perspective, our interest in the future of the world would disappear.

The aim of this essay is to propose a biblical perspective that is grounded in *this* life, in the love of *this* world—not the wish to exist in another universe—and in the hope that the "reign of heaven" will come to *this* world—not the dream to exist in some spiritual world. It assumes that preserving natural life, protecting human beings, and promoting the dignity of human life are worth it. What that means, correspondingly, is that opposing all that threatens life is imperative. Developing a worldview that motivates us to do these things, accordingly, is vital. This is a challenge, we can see, when the dominant worldviews today suggest that there is no hope for life or that we should place our hope in another life.

How should we see what is going on in the world? Looking over the history of the universe, this essay argues that it makes sense to regard its evolution as mindful and purposeful. Yet—in view of the stumbles and stops and destruction along the way, as well as the possible end of the universe—it

---

1. See Halpern, *Allure of the Multiverse*.

is a contested purpose. Seen in this light, we should see the beginning of the cosmos as a deliberate act to deliver the universe from chaos so that it could be free to realize its potential. The purpose of human existence, it follows, is to preserve natural life, protect human beings, and promote human dignity. What gives us hope for this world is the faith that we participate in this ongoing creation and the love—courageous, unselfish love—that can succeed in opposing and defeating the corruption and violence in the world.

WORLDVIEWS

A worldview, or guiding idea of what is going on in the world, serves to orient our lives. It helps us make sense of where we came from and where we are going. It indicates what we know, how we should live, and what we might hope for. For beings like us, with our intelligence, emotional capacities, and volition, it is natural to orient ourselves in the world by trying to understand how we wound up where we did, to forecast where our lives are headed, and to give reasons for how we should live. It is especially important that a worldview explains how it is that humans have the capacity to form a worldview at all, or even to ask the question, "What's really going on in the world?" That in itself is a wonder. If we do not have a worldview that makes sense of where we came from and where we are going, we could not establish worthwhile goals for ourselves, let alone employ those distinctly human capabilities to achieve them; we would, instead, merely pursue one desire after another, winding up in dead ends and ditches, stumbling through life.

What's really going on in the world? As we survey the world before us, how do we characterize what, when all is said and done, is going on in the world? While answers to that question can be simplistic, they can also be telling, indicating what we think is ultimately true, pointing to how we should live, and conveying what we might hope for. For example, we could think that the universe is simply matter randomly coming together and coming apart, and that life is a struggle between living forms vying to survive. If that is our worldview, we would conclude that we can only cope with what life throws at us and just hope (or wish) for whatever happiness happens our way. Or, we could think that this world is really subordinate to another world, a spiritual realm, from which God intervenes to direct events in this world. If we believed that that is what is actually going on in heaven and Earth, we would live our lives in the hope (or dream) that one day God will bring our souls to live in that realm. There are other possible worldviews, of course, but those two, generally speaking, are the most common today in the United States.

How should we characterize what is really going on in the world? Chance and struggle, miracles and spiritual journeys, or something else? We need a worldview that answers that question and that points to where life is headed so that we can give direction to our lives.

When we survey the universe with the widest lens—where we came from, what our world has become, and where it is headed—what do we see? That our world came into existence at all—that matter formed from formless energy, that life emerged from matter, and that humans evolved into beings with minds, hearts, and wills—is a wonder. The very existence of life on Earth is a rare and marvelous development. Its persistence, considering how vulnerable it is and imperiled by hazards, is remarkable.

We know that life is surrounded by many threats, that life itself is precarious. Life persists, remarkably, even as it is surrounded by lifelessness. Life is a marvel; that life can be destroyed so easily and fall back into lifelessness is awful. And when we examine human life with a finer lens—what it has developed out of and what it can descend into—we see that human existence, too, is vulnerable and threatened with destruction. Our worldview—where we came from, what we are, and where we are going—would focus upon these observations, as well as the fact that we are beings who can behold such wonders. We are beings who have the aesthetic capacity to sense the wonderful, the intellect to reflect upon it, and the will to respond to it.

Making sense of how it all began and how it will all end, then, can help explain where we are and where we are going. We also gain insight into what's going on in the universe if we consider what's going on in the middle, as it were. We can look at ourselves—the only beings in the universe (as far as well can tell) who have the ability to wonder about such things—as the high-water mark in the universe. While we could say that the evolution of beings with intelligence, emotions, and free will was random, we must at least assert that it is wonderful—something that compels us to take note of, something that stimulates our intellect to understand, and something we should account for—and not simply a mere random happening, a brute fact, or a baffling curiosity. When we consider the richness of human existence—set between formless voids at the beginning and at the end—we must not be perplexed into silence or say with a shrug of our shoulders, "That's just the way it is," or "That's just the way God planned it." We should be led to consider, rather, that there is a reason for these developments.

Humankind in its short existence, to look more closely, has developed capacities that can both care for life as well as destroy it. On the one hand, humans can give their lives to improve the lives of others, and even sacrifice their lives for other living things—conduct, we should note, often inconsistent with the goal of self-preservation. On the other hand, they push living things into extinction, spoil their own environment, kill one another, and even plot to destroy themselves—conduct more consistent with self-destruction than self-preservation. This, too, is a wonder—one overshadowed by dismay.

How do we account for both the wonderful and the dismaying? Is there "something going on" in life, something mindful or purposeful as well as something chaotic and destructive that helps make sense of this?[2]

There are those who think that they can "get along without any worldview," that they do not need to think through where we have come from, where we are going, what we should do, and what we might hope for. They are not even curious about the answers their forebears gave to those questions. Some even think that "no one really knows anything" about such things so that there are no insights to guide us. They might think, further, that morality is all "subjective and relative" so that they can live however they want to, and that, again, there is no settled wisdom to guide us. They might think, finally, that they can hope for "whatever you wish for." Who, after all, is to say that their dreams can't come true? While many profess such thoughtlessness as a guide to living, in practice, most have a working, if not articulate, worldview. Those who don't will find that a confused, dithering life is the price of such thoughtlessness.

How should we go about constructing a thoughtful worldview today? The sciences provide the best models for discerning what we can know, so our worldview would be guided by scientific methods that assume physical regularities in our world. Our view of the physical world, however, need not draw the *metaphysical* conclusion that our world consists merely of matter, or that the world can be explained simply in terms of it. Such a view does not fully characterize all that there is in the world but leaves unexplained realities we need to give an account of. There is more to our world than matter-in-motion.

Our worldview, furthermore, should draw upon humanity's moral wisdom. Just as our understanding of the natural world has developed since antiquity, so too our understanding of how we should live, or of our moral world, has developed. Just as laws help account for natural life, so too moral rules help us organize human life. Furthermore, a moral view of the world can guide our lives in this world without having to refer to *another* world. It would find the fulfillment of human life in *this* world, not in a future world or in some spiritual existence. We need not introduce an *otherworldly* realm in order to realize the goal of moral living.

2. Throughout his publications in science and religion, Paul Davies expresses the conviction that "something is going on" in the universe that needs accounting for. See *Templeton Prize Address*; *What's Eating the Universe?*, 155–59.

This worldview, finally, should make a reasonable assessment concerning what we can hope for based on our scientific and moral understandings. In order to account for what's going on in the world, it would not, it follows, invoke supernatural causes to intervene in the world, and it need not introduce a spiritual afterlife as the goal of our worldly lives. To anticipate the discussion: this worldview would be based on the understanding the sciences have developed but not reduced to materialism; and it would be guided by moral rules but not commit to theism. It would align these insights concerning where we came from, what we are, and where we are going with a biblical understanding that gives us the faith and hope to live lives of love in a world threatened by destruction.

The objective of this essay is to set out a worldview that orients our lives, points to how we should live, and gives us hope. We need this because the two worldviews commonly held today, materialism and theism, do not help us understand what's really going on in our world, how we should live in it, and what we might hope for. That is to say, if we thought that the world was nothing but matter, we could have no hope for the world, but would resign ourselves to the coming destruction of matter—my own, my species', the Earth's, the universe's. In the case of my own life, if I thought that all living things—including the people around me—were in competition for the resources—the matter—I need to survive, then looking out for others, cooperating with them, sharing with them, caring for them—living morally, in other words—will very often appear imprudent, if not foolish. Or, if I thought that there was a heaven beyond this world, I would place my hope in *that* world and lose wholehearted concern for *this* world. If I thought that my future heavenly existence was of ultimate importance for me, in other words, then moral living would be only a means to that end. I would have ulterior motives for living morally. Either way, my moral life would be inauthentic because it would not be something I do for its own sake—something that is inherently right, in accordance with what is really true about the world and my fellow human beings—but as a means to some other end. Neither materialism nor theism inspire us to live up to our moral dignity or to live in hope for our world.

Living a morally principled life, we can come to see, is worth doing simply because it is inherently the right thing to do, because it accords with the way the world truly is—with what is really going on in the world—not because it can work to my own advantage, or because it shows obedience to God, or establishes a right relationship with God, or earns my way to heaven. It simply rings true for human existence, for our place in the world, quite apart from whether it advantages me in some way. It simply is what there is for human beings to do.

Reflecting upon where we came from and where we are going, to conclude, we should not simply see amazing things that leave us dumbfounded, but wonders that cry out for explanation. The greatest wonder is that we can behold and account for these wonders at all. Our world has existed only briefly between a long, lifeless beginning and what appears will be a long, lifeless end. Furthermore, life is a rarity, balanced precariously between chaotic disorder and inert order. It is a wonder that the world persists even while natural forces—subterranean, terrestrial, and extraterrestrial—imperil and threaten to destroy it. And it would be absolutely dreadful if natural forces destroyed the Earth or life became extinct. Such destruction has not—yet—overtaken the world; instead, the world persists and life is sustained. Can we hope that these wonders will continue? Might we hope that life will spring from lifelessness throughout the universe, or that human beings will advance in their capacities to understand and care for life—even beyond Earth?

Today, knowing what we do about the history of the universe, we might offer a theological worldview that validates our wonder. There is a reason for there being a cosmos and not chaos; for life evolving and flourishing, not devolving and decaying back into lifelessness; and for living things and self-aware, intelligent moral beings. It is because some initiative freed matter from chaos—informing it with laws and driving evolution—that matter could realize its potential. Where there was only unformed potential, now there is evolving life.

We also know, however, that matter could dissolve and disintegrate into a formless void. The whole universe could descend into a state of unceasing chaos, living systems could devolve into a state of permanent lifelessness, and human beings might succumb to corruption and violence, ending civilized life. The reason for this is that disorder works to undermine matter, unravel its development, and corrupt life. Both a providential ordering as well as an incessant disordering contend over matter, both freeing it to develop and subjecting it to confusion, both informing and misinforming it.

In that light, how should we characterize what is really going on in the world? Chance and struggle, miracles and spiritual journeys? We should look at is this way: love and deliverance. Love seeking to deliver the world from chaos.

Biblical theology can assert that it was the love of God that saw a formless, lifeless world bound in darkness, and that breathed life into it, giving of itself in order to free the world so that it could "be fruitful and multiply." So understood, God created the universe not for divine pleasure, not as a show of bountifulness, not to receive the worship of creatures, and not as a first stage or test for humans to make their way to heaven. It was not for any of these reasons but solely out of love for the world. Christian theology, in view of Jesus's life and crucifixion furthermore, would underscore that this love was selfless, dauntless, costly, and successful. In other words, love works.

To say that "God loves the world" or that "God is love" is nothing new for biblical theology. Given the context this essay explores, we would highlight the claim that just as God's love for the world opposed the deep darkness in the beginning, so today it opposes the chaos that menaces the world now and works to free the world from it. An earlier day would have said that God frees the world from "sin, death, and the devil." Today, we might say, more understandably, that such love frees the world from bondage to chaos: the unremitting disorder that, in various ways, undermines life and the conditions for life. Such love opposes this bondage and effectuates that freedom.

If we can believe that love was the power that initiated the creation—wresting matter from chaos and advancing the life-giving in defiance of the life-less—then we can hope that love may prevail in the end. That is biblical faith and hope. It is faith, "the conviction of things not seen" (Heb 11:1)—not a foregone conclusion. It is hope, "hope that is seen is not hope" (Rom 8:24)—not a given. It is hope in the power of love to free from powers of destruction so that the loved, in turn, love others—the fulfillment of creation.

The claim is that the universe exists, life persists, and human dignity is realized only because there is this love that defies the chaos threatening to return everything to nothing. Given the formidable powers in the world working to destroy the world and return it to nothingness, what is required today are acts of undaunted, costly love: help given unselfishly and dearly for life threatened by destruction. Our own experience, furthermore, attests that such love can stand up to and defeat powers of corruption and violence.

A biblical theology, then, claims that it is the love of God that accounts for the creation of the universe from a formless void. The love of God also explains our own capacity to love: to understand the plight of others, to empathize with them, and to free them from their own enslavements. These capacities allow us to see the disorder in the lives of others and to help free them from them. Understood in this way, love is the beginning and the end, the starting point and the culmination of creation.

It was love that succeeded in bringing the universe into being from a formless void and in bringing life out of lifelessness; love that succeeded in bringing the light of consciousness out of the darkness of insensible life; and love that presses us to protect and promote life. Love works. Will it prevail over the chaos that threatens to return everything to a lifeless void? We don't know, though we might hope. But even if the universe disintegrates back into a formless void, even if we irreversibly corrupt life on Earth or destroy civilization, love succeeded. Such destruction will not have made the power of love any less effective. It is because love has been proven to work that we should actively hope in the power of love to protect life on Earth and to sustain the universe. The alternatives—to wish for another universe in a multiverse, or to dream of a heaven to replace Earth—simply surrender to destructive powers threatening to overwhelm our world. Better to hope that love works—to make that leap—than to countenance worldviews that do not actively sustain and promote life, and that even undermine it, hastening its demise.

WHAT CAN WE KNOW? WHAT OUGHT WE DO? WHAT MIGHT WE HOPE?

To articulate such a worldview, we might pose these three questions, as the Enlightenment philosopher Kant did: What can we know? What ought we do? What might we hope? How would we answer these questions today? Much has changed in the nearly 250 years since the Enlightenment. Most significantly, our increased knowledge of the natural world combined with our technical ability to shape the world that stems from that knowledge—for good and ill—orients our worldview today.

What can we know? The sciences provide the best models for discerning what we can know. The methods they use, the regularities they find, and the laws they formalize enable us to gain a better and better understanding of the world. If we deny these insights, it is hard to imagine how we could establish an objective, comprehensive worldview. If "scientists don't know anything," we have no common ground to form our expectations for the future and to direct our lives. It is discouraging that so many people have that opinion. Unable to distinguish fact from fantasy, or to discriminate what's merely possible from what's very likely, or to separate private preference from objective evidence, they cannot get a grip on what's really going on in the world because all possible perspectives are in play and all futures are up for grabs. Then there can be no common ground to develop a worldview that establishes a comprehensive point of view and shared concerns. No coordinated, sustained enterprises would be possible.

A similar opinion afflicts the thinking of many concerning our knowledge of our social world, or the human context we live in. That is the opinion that we cannot distinguish true beliefs from false beliefs, virtual reality from reality itself, information from disinformation, facts from alternate facts. But if there is no difference between real information and *mis*information—distracting, incorrect, and misleading information—and *dis*information—deceptive, dishonest, and intentionally false information—then all human relationships will be jeopardized. We could not trust our communications or rely on our contracts. Our ability to communicate, to come to a common understanding, and to form agreements would break apart. In social contexts, where unprincipled and malevolent actors threaten to do harm, it is vital to distinguish the truth from lies. Here we might learn a lesson from the natural world: misinformation can be fatal. Mutations stemming from faulty or misread genetic information, for example, can lead to malignancies and fatal diseases; and it is often through disinformation, or by concealing their identities, that deadly viruses attack and destroy healthy cells.

The answer to the question "What ought we do?" will draw upon humanity's moral wisdom. That inherited wisdom has been distilled into the common moral rule "do to others as you would have them do to you." This means, more fully, that we ought to preserve life, protect human beings, and promote human dignity. We all know, in fact, that the world would be a better place if we followed that rule. Knowing that the future of the world may be bleak, however, we are tempted to dismiss that rule and to revise our answer to the question, "What ought we do?" We might be tempted to answer instead, "Eat, drink, and be merry, for tomorrow we die," or "Wait upon the next life." Why be concerned for—let alone expend myself for—life that has no future or ideals that can never be realized? We will see, on the contrary, that the so-called golden rule holds true now as it did in the Enlightenment as well as in ancient cultures, the biblical world in particular.

We now know that Earth and the life on it evolved from lifelessness, and that lifelessness could be its final end. This knowledge, that the short-term future of life on Earth is precarious and that the long-term future is bleak, places the question "What might we hope for?" in a troubling context. The best way to give a credible answer to that question today, ironically, is to reference something primeval. It is something that we ignore (as many Enlightenment thinkers did), though biblical authors pondered. In view of what is going on in the world, the best way to articulate how it is that the universe is disintegrating and the world is being pulled into lifelessness is to posit a disordering that threatens to destroy the world. This is a new reality (for us) that we need to face and contend with. Only by doing so can we realistically address the question, "What might we hope for?"

What, then, might we hope? Today we have the knowledge and the means to turn back many of the destructive forces menacing us; the question is whether we have the will to act on them. We also know that the way to thwart the corruption and violence humanity faces is to follow moral rules known to all; the question is whether we have the courage to live according to them since it will be perilous and costly to do so. Faith that a purposeful plan and a loving will is active in the universe can inspire us to live in hope that life can be sustained, even that the universe will be saved from destruction. Such faith is not certainty because we do not know whether or not destruction will have the last word in the universe or in human existence. Given the destructive forces at work in the universe and the corruption and violence in our world, it will require a leap of hope to embrace that worldview. The question is whether we will take that leap and live in that faith, or whether we will let destructive forces at work in the world go unopposed.

What can we know? What ought we do? What might we hope? Organizing this discussion around these three questions traverses the territory a worldview needs to cover. Because we are circling the globe from different angles and heights, answering them will produce an overlapping or layering result, and, we expect, a consistent and complete outlook on life that guides how we ought to live.

PART ONE

I

What Can We Know?

THE WORLD IS HEADED FOR DESTRUCTION. WHY?

The Bible begins with darkness enshrouding the Earth. In the beginning of the Christian Scriptures, in the Gospel according to John, darkness opposes the light that comes into the world. That conflict comes to a decisive point when corrupt and violent men execute Jesus as darkness covered the Earth. To account for the way our world is today, similarly, it makes sense to start with the darkness pervading it. We see its manifestations in the dark energy pulling the cosmos apart, in lethal mutations and fatal diseases prematurely ending life; we observe it in the cruelties afflicting human life, and we witness it in the destructive human heart. Such darkness is real and active throughout the world, and, in the end, may overwhelm all the light and life in it.

From the very large to the very small, our world is teetering toward destruction. The universe is disintegrating. Protons—the basis of all the matter in the universe—are decaying. The star that gives life to Earth will expand, explode, and incinerate Earth. Life on Earth, furthermore, is threatened by destruction from several directions. Extraterrestrial hazards such as asteroids and cosmic radiation as well as subterranean convulsions such as volcanoes and earthquakes may doom life on Earth. Environmental challenges of various kinds also threaten all forms of life with extinction. Why is this? Did the Creator plan for the creation to self-destruct? Long before these things happen, finally, we may destroy ourselves. The only intelligent beings known in the universe produce tools, weapons, and waste that threaten their own lives as well as all life on their own planet. Why would creatures act that way? All this suggests the presence of a pervasive chaos disordering the cosmos, confusing our souls, and it recalls the darkness depicted by the biblical authors.

Is all this simply happenstance, or can we generalize from these observations? Can we draw connections between what we might call cosmic chaos at one end of the spectrum and moral evil at the other? Can we ask, when we see a disintegrating universe, natural deformities, and human destructiveness, whether there is a common origin sowing such disorder? We need to ask the question: How is it that our ordered, life-giving world, arising from a chaotic beginning, seems destined for a disordered, lifeless end? We can't avoid this issue by saying "That's just the way the world is" because that would leave us disoriented and directionless. From formlessness comes form, from lifelessness comes life, from the insensible comes self-awareness; yet all seems destined to fall back into a dark, formless void forever. Why is this? Even more in need of explanation is why intelligent human beings who understand these things, who are products of and beneficiaries of this ordered world, and who can support and nurture it nonetheless disrupt it and even threaten their own existence. Why is this? Perhaps the darkness pointed to in the Bible helps provide an answer.

Before developing the idea that a real darkness, chaos, or void threatens the world, we should note two common responses—one philosophical, one theological—that discount the objective reality of darkness and dismiss an active source for disorder. The first objection maintains that the universe is nothing but matter. There are no souls, no God, no darkness. If the human species commits suicide, if life on Earth is extinguished, if the universe wastes away—even if all these things happen—this is simply due to matter's innate properties. It had to happen that way just because material things do those things. There is little more to be said. On the second view as well, the darkness is not real. The Creator, the creation, and heaven are real, but cosmic chaos, natural evils, and human sin have been or will be dispersed, overcome, or redeemed so that, in the end, God "may be all in all" (1 Cor 15:28). Darkness, on this account, is only temporary, or the absence of light, or simply serves some greater good, or is allowed because God—who "make[s] weal and create[s] woe" (Isa 45:7)—permits it.

Both views—call them philosophical materialism and traditional theism—have been dominant worldviews in the West, but neither provide adequate answers to our questions. We need better reasons to account for this troubling feature of the universe than "the unfathomable will of God" or "a brute inexplicable fact." The first is not believable anymore. The second is no answer at all. What is it about our universe that leads to this end? Is there some corrosive influence or destructive pressure that contributes to its demise? There must be reasons for these circumstances that we can understand at least in part and that help orient us concerning how to live in what appears to be a doomed world.

Suppose the darkness *is* real: an active, objective, independent reality, not merely a figurative or subjective way of talking about reality. Maybe it is not simply a disagreeable, inexplicable characteristic of the world—a brute aspect of matter or a mysterious creation of the Creator we must accept—but a threat to the world we should confront and oppose. Maybe, to put it another way, the darkness is not something we have to accept, like the dark tiles in a mosaic that provide contrast in a beautiful picture, or the tragic episodes in a story that are offset by a good ending, but something we should reject and fight—like a cancer that threatens to kill me. In this way of thinking, darkness is real, active, and lethal. It is not just an unfortunate quality of matter or an inevitable shadow in an otherwise good creation. It stems from an independent source that sows chaos and that threatens to return life to lifelessness, blotting out the light that sustains our world. As such, the darkness is something we should oppose, and perhaps that light and life can overcome.[1]

The darkness is real, but so is the light. We have to account for that as well. The power of corruption and destructiveness are real, but so is the persistence of life and love. We do not dwell in lifeless darkness alone; and it is sensible to think there are reasons both for the life-supporting order in the cosmos as well as life-threatening chaos. From lifeless matter comes living things and even conscious beings—beings who can comprehend the evolution of life and even alter it. How do we explain this? Biblical writers believed that it was the Word or Spirit of God that instilled ordering principles, breathing life into lifeless matter. Human beings, moreover, not only comprehend the evolution of life and understand the drive for self-preservation, but they can override them by self-giving, by giving over their

---

1. Next to Christianity, C. S. Lewis thought that dualism was the "most sensible creed on the market," and that Christianity is much "nearer to Dualism than people think." *Mere Christianity*, 48, 50. Lewis thinks of dualism in terms of two beings fighting each other, one good, one bad. But because the bad being has "intelligence and will," which are good things, "he must be getting both from the Good Power," so that "Dualism, in a strict sense, will not work." The approach taken here does not think of the Creator as a supreme being, or of creation *ex nihilo* (from the absence of anything), or of the bad power as a being "who likes badness for its own sake." The approach here hopes to account for the destructive disorder in our world that fits with our contemporary understanding, as well as with biblical themes.

lives for the sake of other life. How do we account for this? Biblical writers believed that it was the love of God that made this possible.

Biblical authors gave us concepts and stories to guide our thinking concerning the origin and destiny of the universe, but they had little knowledge of the natural world. Given our current understanding, what explanation makes sense for us? It is incumbent upon intelligent beings to give an account that helps orient their place in the world, that explains both why there is this orderliness that makes the universe—and our understanding of it—possible, as well as how it is that disorder may destroy everything in the end. There is orderliness but also opposition to this orderliness, opposition of such magnitude that it could obliterate the natural world, leaving only an unending state of chaos. How can this be, and how are we to live in such a world? We should not let our wonder and dread before this state of affairs go unaddressed.

The Bible addresses this wonder by claiming that the Creator entered into the darkness and opposed it by drawing a world from out of primeval, chaotic waters, breathing life into human beings, freeing them from corruption and violence, and ultimately saving humanity so that they could be stewards of the world, servants of one another, even "children of God" (1 John 3:1). This insurgent God aimed to free us—and the whole creation—from all that enslaves and suppresses so that we might realize our potential, developing our capacities to love one another as God loved the world. It is because God loved the world that God freed it from chaos and—at great cost, according to the Christian Scriptures—freed humanity from bondage to self-love and violence so that they too might love the world. That is what God is doing in the universe: freeing from lifelessness and destructiveness for life and love.

God entered into the darkness, opposed it, and equipped humanity to do the same. Human beings have the rational capacity to understand the world, to recognize what is destructive and perceive what is good, as well as the willpower to act on our knowledge of good and evil. We also have emotions, with their powers of empathy, forgiveness, and love, to confront the darkness in our world and in ourselves—powers that can break though the darkness that shrouds human life in corruption and violence.

These elements from the Bible can form the basis for a theological worldview today. Theology lifts up key elements in the biblical account and aligns them with our contemporary perspective. These connections and this congruence can enlighten our understanding and orient our lives in the world by giving a coherent explanation of what is really going on in the world. The aim of this essay is to show that biblical theology provides a worldview that moves us to oppose the darkness, have faith in the light, and live in hope and love. Unlike many religions and philosophies today, it will not promise a comfortable worldview, and it will conflict with the view that the goal of life is the "pursuit of happiness." It will not offer a world-escaping "spiritual life" or provide "a spiritual relationship with God," but it will ground our lives more firmly in our natural, moral lives. In confronting a troubling truth about life—that the darkness is real—this worldview seeks to account for it, orient our lives to face up to it, and inspire faith, hope, and love to challenge it.

We know a great deal about our world. We have discovered laws that explain its structures, and we understand the delicate balances that make life possible. We can even employ those laws to preserve and promote life, as well as predict how, in the end, disorder may extinguish life. That the world has such order, that we can understand it, and that we can help sustain it is an awe-inspiring wonder. It is also a wonder, a frightful wonder, that we can foresee disorder obliterating our world and preview our own demise. The ordering that makes possible a cosmos, living things, and intelligent beings—beings who can care for life and each other—at the same time is threatened by disorder—both natural and human—that could turn everything back into a lifeless chaos forever. A theological account may best explain this.

The aim, then, is to develop a theological account that assumes the development of the universe as we know it and that provides an explanation for its origin and destiny. From beginning to end, this, in brief, is its course as we currently know it: out of formless energy emerged an orderly cosmos capable of supporting life and self-conscious beings, only to waste away and return to formless energy. It is a movement from formless energy with great potential to formless energy with no potential. Looking back over this course from end to beginning, it may appear to be a completely useless waste. It is a movement from energy—frozen in time, going nowhere—to useless radiation going nowhere. In between, though, there is the development of complex forms of energy, the evolution of self-directed living things, and finally the emergence of beings who can understand this movement, shape its direction, and act for both good and evil. From our human point of view, the most advanced we are aware of, we see a sweep up from formless, directionless potential to self-aware beings purposefully directing their futures, capable both of heedlessly putting the wellbeing of others before their own as well as needlessly destroying others. A theological account may explain these movements, orient us in the universe, and guide our lives in it.

A number of elements in the biblical worldview align with our contemporary perspective. At the start of the creation, biblical authors wrote that "the earth was a formless void and darkness covered the face of the deep" (Gen 1:2).[2] It would be congruent with our current understanding to say that we start with energy in a state of chaos. Energy, or perhaps pure potential, is present in a featureless, formless state. It is frozen in that state, we might add, because a deep darkness prevents it from actualizing its potential—from becoming ordered, diverse, and complex—keeping energy in a state of chaos such that a cosmos could not develop. Then the authors continue: "[The spirit of] God swept over the face of the waters." The Spirit that moved against the chaos and the light that broke into the darkness, we might elaborate, initiated the laws and imparted the information that gave form to formless potential by informing it, ordering it with regularities that are lawlike, consistent, and dependable so that a cosmos emerged from chaos, and eventually living things and conscious beings.

After God dispersed the darkness, formed the world, brought forth living things and eventually human beings, the biblical account continues, God protected human beings from the darkness of corruption and violence. The biblical writers were stunned, as we should be, with our love of violence, and with our desire, unlike anything in the animal world, to choose death over life. At the same time, they realized that our capacities for reasoning, empathizing, and tending to the creation give us dignity and responsibilities exceeding the animals. They tried to account for this. While we would not explain our willingness to choose death over life, as well as our knowledge of good and evil, as the result of a fateful encounter with a talking snake, we too should wonder both at how cruel humans can be as well as how loving.

God enlightened human beings, the biblical account continues, by giving moral laws, inspiring wisdom, and sending prophets to steer humanity away from corruption and violence and onto the path of justice and love. Besides the biblical tradition, we should note, many others over the millennia have acknowledged a fundamental moral law, the "golden rule," that directs us to treat others as we ourselves want to be treated. This rule comes so naturally to beings with our rational and emotional capacities that it is as if it were "written on our hearts," to which our "conscience also bears witness" (Rom 2:15). Throughout the ages, humans have recognized that we should

---

2. Biblical writers and both Jewish and Christian theologians (such as Philo, Rashi, Justin Martyr, and Hermogenes) held that God created the world from existing stuff. It was not until Christians saw the need to assert the absolutely unconditioned nature of creation and the absolute sovereignty and freedom of God that the doctrine of creation *ex nihilo* took hold. See May, *Creatio Ex Nihilo*. Jon Levinson explains, "It seems more likely that they identified 'nothing' with things like disorder, injustice, subjugation, disease, and death. To them, in other words, 'nothing' was something—something negative." Regarding God's absolute power, he writes that this is "realizing itself in achievement and relationship" and that this is "omnipotence *in potentia*." *Creation and the Persistence of Evil*, xxi, xvi.

follow this moral law; nevertheless, too often we ignore it, spurn that path, and even choose death instead. Why is this? The biblical account maintains that it was because we "loved darkness rather than light" (John 3:19). Even though we have the potential—the reason, the compassion, and the willpower—to be merciful, forgive, and love, we do not realize that potential; we do not order our lives according to the moral law but leave that potential undeveloped, and we remain mired in animosity, corruption, and violence. We love the darkness and surround ourselves with it.

To elaborate, on the one hand, we come to realize that all persons have dignity, that we ought to show them the respect we ourselves deserve, and that the world would be a better place if we did. Even though such regard for others may run counter to our instincts for self-preservation and may prove costly to us, we understand that we owe it to each other to treat one another this way and that we can do this. On the other hand, we are tempted to let animosities get the better of us, to do harm to others, and, strangest of all, to do harm to ourselves. We attack other living things needlessly with a savagery unknown in the animal world. How do we account for our seeming "unnatural" ability both to do good out of love and do evil out of hate? Neither are natural tendencies of other living things. The biblical answer is that it is the love of God that turns us outside of ourselves and toward others, loving them as we love ourselves and as God loved the world; but also, it is the power of darkness that turns us against others, tempting us to harm them and ourselves. Not wanting to be stewards of the world and caregivers of one another as we were created to be, we want, instead, to be "like God" (Gen 3:5) and turn away from our moral calling.

Finally, just as God broke through the chaos, formed a world out of the formless void, and pushed the darkness away to create a world, in the Gospel according to Mark, God tears apart the heavens to save a world shrouded in the darkness of corruption and violence by sending the Messiah. Jesus enters into the world to usher in God's reign of mercy, forgiveness, and love. But the world did not accept him; instead, it rejected and killed him. The Christian Scriptures conclude with the conviction that that was not the end for Jesus, but that he continued to live in his communities, imparting his spirit of mercy, forgiveness, and love to all humankind. Life in his spirit is true human life and gives power to overcome the darkness of corruption and violence.

The consistent message in the Bible is that God frees humanity—even the whole world—*from* bondage to darkness *for* freedom, the freedom to love one another as God loved the world. Hebrew authors believed that the natural and moral orders God instituted to hold back chaotic waters and to restrain corruption and violence would prevail; Christian authors believed that God's love for the world was self-giving and costly. They knew this from Jesus's life and death as well as from the life and persecution of their own communities. They hoped, nevertheless, that the love of God would not fail but prevail through them.

Biblical writers had hope that the love of God would reign through all humanity and even over the whole world because they had faith in the power of that love. To believe that, and to live in that love, was a risk—it was a leap of hope—because it was far from evident that love would win in the end, especially when prophets were killed, the Messiah was executed, and believers persecuted. From our vantage point, if the creation ends in feeble, useless radiation—not even dust—as many cosmologists forecast, it may be hard to think anything other than that chaos—not the love of God—prevails in the end. Even if there are other worlds—now and yet to come—or a heaven, *this* creation came to nothing. It is hard to think that the Creator, who loved the creation and declared it "very good," also planned its annihilation. Or, if human beings destroy themselves and doom the lives of other creatures, it is hard to think that it was the love of the Creator that dwelt in their hearts, but something else: the love of darkness or chaos. What would it mean today to have faith that the love of the Creator will sustain the creation in face of the darkness that threatens it? Do we take the leap to live in the light and to risk our lives to love the creation and its creatures as the Creator did, or do we prefer to dwell in the darkness, allowing it to snuff out all life and love?

There is some reason to think that there could be a future for the universe other than a formless void. Perhaps there is more potential in the universe—the 95 percent of matter and energy we do not know about—that will support life and self-conscious beings and will persist over disorder. Scientists will learn more and find out. Or perhaps there is reason to hope in the matter and energy we know intimately—ourselves. When we consider humanity's achievements, we might have hope that our capabilities can succeed in protecting, preserving, and promoting life and will withstand the darkness that tempts us and threatens the world. Most especially, when we consider our own lives and realize the power of love to overcome obstacles like resentments, animosities, and ill will, we might believe that love will prevail in the end, just as the love of God overcame darkness in the beginning.

The darkness is real. Asserting its reality helps us account for the formless chaos at the beginning, and why it may be there at the end. It is the reason the universe is headed toward destruction. Like the deep, dark waters present at the beginning of the biblical account, chaos threatens to inundate the cosmos, returning it to a void. Looking at our own world, we know how fragile life on Earth is, and we know how abruptly natural forces—and how directly human actions—could destroy it. To preserve living things and to protect human life, we need to face the darkness that threatens them and to oppose it; otherwise, corruption and violence may destroy us.

We need a worldview that confronts this reality. Materialism, claiming that matter is all there is, does little more than point out the ways matter interacts with other matter, causing us either pain or pleasure. Not even an enlightened materialism, one that nudges us to protect our environment out of self-interest, can inspire us to do what needs to be done given the threats we face. Even though an enlightened materialism might realize how foolish it is to spoil our own nest, why should we be concerned about what happens to the environment after we die? We might do what is necessary to preserve our own lives from destruction, but why should we be concerned about—let alone sacrifice for—future lives, for lives we will never know? Wouldn't that only distract us from our avoidance of pain and pursuit of pleasure? Similarly, if our religious belief was that a future life in heaven is what should concern us, why would we be concerned about—let alone sacrifice for—the future of life on Earth? Neither worldview inspires us to confront the challenges before us.

Surveying the darkness around us and in us, considering what it will take to preserve life on Earth as well as keep corruption and violence from destroying us, we can see that philosophies or religious beliefs based on self-preservation or self-interest or happiness—now or in a hereafter—are not adequate. They are actually part of the problem because they take our attention away from the darkness threatening our world and place it instead on ourselves. Facing up to the darkness and opposing it, though, will take us outside of our own self-interests. It will demand our devoted attention, take time and effort, and it will be costly. Turning our attention to the needs of our world is difficult because it disrupts our pursuit of happiness. From the biblical point of view, we need to be turned away from the temptation to stand idly by in the face corruption and violence and away from idle pursuits of happiness. We need, rather, to be turned outside of ourselves toward others. From the biblical point of view, faith in God who loved the world accomplishes this turn, inspires hope, and impels us to love others.

Facing up to these challenges requires the will to utilize the capacities that equip us to do so. Neither materialism nor traditional theism do that. Neither encourage us to exert ourselves to oppose the darkness threatening life on Earth since they tempt us to believe that either matter or God have determined the future of life on Earth. Both abdicate the very freedom required to put those capacities into action. But why, we must ask, are human beings fit to steward life on Earth and to care for each other? The truth is that we have the capacity to look beyond ourselves: we have an eye for the needs of others, we can see into the future, and we are free to act on those insights. Let's not be beguiled into believing we don't or shouldn't. Let's not pretend that we are merely material beings struggling to survive like the rest of the animals, or that we are really angelic beings simply passing through Earth on the way to heaven. Perhaps, rather, there is a reason we are equipped to oppose the darkness. It is more constructive to believe that there is a reason we are this way, namely that our existence is the result of an initiative that is mindful, willful, and even empathetic. It is far better to believe that these capacities are the enactment of a plan aimed to free matter and release its potential for life, most notably life that is intelligent, free, and loving. They stem from an initiative that itself opposes the darkness and frees matter for life and love.

We can pretend we are beings whose destiny is determined by material necessity or divine will, but the truth is that we are free. In human beings, matter has leapt to act on its own initiative. Thanks to the initiative of a mindful will, we are free to use our own. In us, life leaps forward so that we can be stewards of life and caregivers for one another. Many factors, though, tempt us to deny these responsibilities. We can be lulled into thinking that we are either pushed around by material forces or led by the invisible hand of God to a determined outcome. Whenever we fail to live up to our responsibilities and want excuses for our behavior, then, especially, it is convenient to believe that we are simply pawns on planet Earth.

The temptation to abdicate our position as stewards of life and caregivers for one another, playing instead the role of pawns helplessly moved about, is powerful for many. Of course there are forces in play that can overpower us, but they rarely simply cancel us. And if we do not assume our responsibilities to challenge them, we play into the hands of those forces that sow confusion and disorder, pulling us back into the chaos from which we were freed.

It is incumbent upon beings like us to answer the question, "Why is the world the way it is?" When we do, we make an important observation: it is remarkable that we can even ask this question. How do we account for the capacities that give us the vantage point even to pose it? To answer that question, we can do better than simply say that the capacities that allow us to ask that question—let alone answer it and act on it—are an accident, a product of an unaccountable swirling of matter, or that they are predetermined by divine edict. It would be difficult to explain how we have self-consciousness and can act as free, responsible beings—not just instinctual animals—if we are merely products of random matter in motion. It is also difficult to explain how we are free agents—not just puppets—if we are created out of nothing by an omnipotent, omniscient deity. There must be a better way to account for our ability to intelligently ask, truthfully answer, and freely act on questions such as "Where have we come from?," "Where are we going?," and, accordingly, "How should we live?" It would be an account that fully engages those capacities and thereby shows how we might reach, as well as fall short of, our proper place in the world.

As far as we can see, our rational, emotional, and volitional capacities uniquely equip us to learn about the world so that we can act to protect it, preserve it, perhaps improve it, and, in general, live responsible lives in it. It is reasonable to think that they are the result of an ordering that has succeeded in bringing about beings who are able to discern where they came from and where they were going and to act on that understanding. We will account for our rational, emotional, and volitional capacities better if we see that they are the result of an unfolding plan to free energy—primeval energy captive to disorder—so that it might realize its potential for life and love. When we observe how the universe evolves—energy actualizing its potential in identifiable directions—we are led to propose that something purposive is going on.

Let us see, then, whether we have reason to think that the emergence of self-conscious beings was neither an accident nor an edict but the working out of a purposeful—though contested—plan emerging over time. It is reasonable to think that the evolution of our capacities has an origin and that that initiative continues to be active throughout the material world and in us. This plan indicates purposefulness, mindfulness, willfulness, even empathy. It is the result, from the biblical point of view, of love that aims to free matter mired in chaos so that it can develop its potential for life and love. We can account for our rational and moral capacities if they are the result of a wise and caring plan working its way through matter. Our ability to understand our world, to empathize with others, and to act freely may well arise from a purposeful ordering active in the beginning, aiming to raise up beings who can protect life and actively love. These capacities give us freedom to live "above" animal life and to follow moral principles.

But this plan faces opposition. It may be overturned or not realize its goal. It may even fail because we do not use our capacities or use them for destructive purposes. Too often we do not exercise those capacities but live "beneath" them, choosing corruption and violence instead, acting with savagery and cruelty not present in the animal world. Why is this? It is because those capacities are tempted by destructiveness, by the lure of disorder and chaos. It is because, as the writer of Genesis put it, "sin is lurking at the door" (Gen 4:7). Biblical writers knew that the darkness was within us as well as outside of us, for "the inclination of the human heart is evil from youth" (Gen 8:21). The darkness is not only real out there but also in here.

THE WORLD IS HEADED FOR DESTRUCTION. WHY SHOULD WE CARE?

It looks as though the universe is disintegrating. Matter itself appears to be wasting away and eventually will be no more. Why is this? Is it simply a brute, inscrutable fact of nature? Is it the Creator's design? The explanation for why the universe is self-destructing, or decaying into nothing, should be better than that this is "just the way it is" or that it is "God's plan." There should be a better answer to that question, one that doesn't simply resign itself to the nature of matter or to supernatural predestining, acquiescing to the demise of the world and the dominion of nothingness, but one that presses for an explanation that orients our lives. A better answer would explain where we came from and where we are going in a way that directs how we should live and what we can hope for.

That answer, we suggested in the last section, considered that the disorder threatening the universe is the result of a corrupting and disrupting influence. Biblical authors, we noted, pointed to the presence of a deep darkness menacing the creation. Paul, for example, thought that creaturely existence was "subjected to futility" and was in "bondage to decay" (Rom 8:20, 21). Why was this? He thought that it was God who subjected the creation to decay in the hope that it would be saved. For reasons we will develop, today we should consider a different theological explanation, one that gives a more active role to "the cosmic powers of this present darkness" (Eph 6:12). In light of our current cosmological understanding, we might develop that concept in order to explain the apparent futility of the universe and why it appears headed toward a pointless ending. We might consider, then, that it is chaos that subjects the cosmos to decay, threatening to destroy it. If that is true, we need to turn from ways of living that do not face up to that or that play-into it. Even more, we need to embrace a way of living that opposes it and that works to sustain life and support humanity. That is the perspective we will begin to develop in this section.

Suppose, though, to step back for a moment, we thought that it really was the nature and destiny of matter to waste away and disintegrate, whether that be a brute fact of nature or the will of God. If that were so, how would we regard the material world, and how would we value it? Wouldn't it be a waste of time to work to preserve a decaying world? Striving to sustain life on Earth, in that case, would be pointless, and the aspiration to extend human life beyond the Earth would be futile. Since matter will not endure, all our effort will come to nothing, and human beings could not plan to accomplish anything lasting on the Earth or beyond it. For believers as well, the call to "prepare the way of the Lord" (Isa 40:3) would ring hollow: we cannot build toward anything because nothing will be left to build on. Why devote our lives to build a future when the present is decaying around us, when the building materials themselves are wasting away?

If all our endeavors to make the world a better place will prove futile, why invest in any? Then the best we could hope for in our material existence would be a bit of happiness. The prudent course would be to live for the moment, enjoying it while we can, rather than build toward a future that is headed for destruction. There is, after all, always more I can do to preserve my life by securing it from dangers and risks, and more I can do to be happy. My interests would probably extend to concern for family and friends because they are important for my security and happiness, but it would make no sense to be concerned about the lives of strangers or those who will live in the future. Given the dangers menacing me in the near future and the futility of life in the long run, it would make no sense at all to risk my life for others, let alone sacrifice for the lives of strangers who will live after me. Because the material world has no future, and because my own material existence is running down and could abruptly end, the prudent thing for me would be to protect my life the best I could. Or, if I thought that there was another, spiritual life after this material world wasted away, I might use this life to gain access to it. In that case, I would treat it simply as a stepping stone to a more valuable, spiritual existence. Either way, there would be no reason to care for the future of life on Earth. Both paths, moreover, given the active disordering present in the world, would only contribute to the neglect and abuse of this world, hastening its demise.

Suppose, though, that the nature and destiny of matter is not to waste away and come to nothing. Suppose the correct understanding of biblical hope is for a future where this material world develops to sustain life and supports beings who can care for it. Suppose that it has the potential to endure, not only to generate beings who can care for it and for each other, but who can build a better future—even "prepare the way of the Lord." A dominant biblical theme, of course, is that the kingdom of God will come to the *Earth*. Earth will be saved and sustained—not destroyed and replaced by heaven, as many Christians suppose. While it may be true, then, that the universe appears headed toward oblivion, this is not because it is the nature of matter to disintegrate or because God planned it that way; it is due, rather, to continual disordering that is real and active in the world. The reason the material world is wasting away is not due to its inherent or created nature, but because it is captive to powers subjecting it to decay. If that is true, how should we live and what might we hope for?

The aim of this essay, to recall, is to show how a biblical theology provides a worldview that prompts us to oppose such darkness and live in faith, hope, and love. It proposes a faith that is thoughtful and enlightened by our contemporary understanding. It moves us to a love that does not seek its own happiness but the welfare of others, and it encourages a courageous love that is not self-serving but unselfish and self-forgetting. Such a contemporary biblical theology gives genuine hope for this world. Because it confronts the darkness surrounding us, it does not promise happiness in this life or another; but, by facing up to the challenges before us in solidarity with others and inspired by the source that first challenged the darkness, it promises a "peace which surpasses all understanding" (Phil 4:7).

Who cares about the future of life on Earth? In one hundred years, after we and all the people we know are gone, why should we care about what happens to our planet? Would those whose lives are defined by the pursuit of happiness care? That's not likely. Why would what happens to the Earth concern them after their pursuits are over? How about those who believe that their final destination is heaven or some other spiritual existence? There's no reason they would care either since they are leaving this world for a better place. For those who look no further than the pursuit of happiness or who look so much further that their ultimate concern is life after this life, it is difficult to see what interest they have in Earth's future. Environmentalists care, of course, though the future of our planet in the long term may well convert their care into despair. Biblical faith, though, gives hope for the world when other worldviews do not, and it inspires the faithful to care for its future.

Given the way many live today, particularly the way we waste resources and the waste we produce, it is evident that many people live only with the span of their own lives in view. The inaction of governments around the world, as well as the slow response of many religions, show that these life-threatening problems prompt little concern. We cannot help but conclude that few care about what will happen to life on Earth. We only care about these problems insofar as they directly affect us; if we can avoid calamity now and push the consequences of our action and inaction on to future generations, we will. It is for our own lives that we live, and perhaps for some future life—not for those who will live after us.

We know, though, that unless we actively care for the future of life on Earth, a number of catastrophes could erupt in the next one hundred years and abruptly end life as we know it. More definitely, we know that inaction on environmental problems, carelessness with nuclear weapons, thoughtless innovations in genetic manipulation and artificial intelligence, or all these things together could lead to our destruction, if not in our own lifetimes then in the life of the next generation. Darkness could descend on our civilization, dispatching us to a brutish existence from which we might never recover, canceling thousands of years of hard-fought progress.[3]

Thoughtful readers of the Bible will care about the future of life on Earth, and they will have hope for its future. Why? Because they understand that they are to be stewards of life on Earth, not behave like animals who only struggle to survive or like angels-in-waiting who continually look to heaven. They have faith, furthermore, that God loves the world and hope that God aims to save it from the darkness that threatens it. Thoughtful readers of the Bible also realize that if we do not care for the future of life on Earth, there likely will not be one because if we simply live for our own lives now or for some future heaven, we abdicate our stewardship of the Earth and leave life vulnerable to the chaos threatening to destroy it.

What kind of thinking, what misguided worldviews, led so many to act as if life on Earth will no longer exist in one hundred years? What could lead us to be so reckless and so destructive in our behavior, flouting the darkness? Such disregard for the future of life on Earth exposes flawed moral understanding, archaic religious worldviews, and wishful metaphysical thinking. It is certainly flawed moral thinking when we fail to apply our fundamental moral principle—that we should do to others as we would have them do to us—to those who will inherit the Earth. It is archaic religious thinking when we uncritically accept the idea that God will destroy the world and then bring us to heaven when our sojourn on Earth is over. And it is wishful metaphysical thinking to believe that we will continue to exist in another universe or some spiritual realm after we die. When we fail to see that future generations deserve our concern, or when we believe that God will destroy the world, or when we blithely anticipate that we will "pass on" to the "next life" where "new experiences" await us, it is no wonder that the end of life on Earth does not trouble us.

Something is dreadfully wrong with worldviews that so poorly orient our lives, leading us into this perilous existence, having such little regard for what will happen to life after we are gone. From the biblical point of view, a deeper explanation—or temptation—lies beneath our disregard for the future of life on Earth. Like Adam and Eve, we are tempted to be something we're not. Instead of being stewards of the Earth and caregivers of life, we'd rather pretend we're "like God." We want to live like gods who can pursue

---

3. For an assessment of these threats, see Ord, *Precipice*. For an assertion of our responsibilities, see MacAskill, *What We Owe*.

happiness with no regard for death and with no moral constraints. We want to be able to pursue happiness in this life and then live on to pursue happiness in a future life, doing whatever we want without being subject to rules or judgments. We want, in other words, to be immortal and amoral. Instead of living like human beings who die and who are responsible for their lives, we want to live like gods who never die and who only follow their own desires.

But we are, in fact, human beings, subject to natural death and to moral rules, though we would rather not be. Both death and responsibilities burden our lives, and we are tempted to think that we would be better off—pursue happiness more freely—without them; and we imagine we can. For one, we are tempted to think we can live forever simply by desiring to: if I want an afterlife of my own dreams, who is to say that that won't come true? It's possible, isn't it? Besides that, it makes me happy to think that new experiences await me after I die. No one should deny me those comforts. Moral responsibilities, furthermore, cause distress because being subject to moral rules often make me feel guilty. That makes me unhappy, and I would rather unburden myself of them. That is easy to do today because many voices entice us to think that there are no real, objective moral standards ordering our lives. We think, instead, that moral rules are subjective, or relative to time and place. Therefore, I can make them up, change them, and drop them as I choose. If I "break" one of my self-imposed "rules," I shouldn't be hard on myself or "beat myself up" but forgive myself or simply change my standards. That would make me happier. Or, if I am religious and believe that breaking moral rules breaks God's law, displeasing God, I simply ask God for forgiveness. God will always forgive me, strengthening my relationship with God. In all these ways I convince myself not to take my mortal, moral life too seriously.

From the biblical point of view, the real reason we act as if Earth no longer exists after we die is that we are tempted to live like gods. We would rather not live like humans—mortal and moral beings responsible for life on Earth—but like gods who are above mortality and morality, who think they can live like immortal, amoral deities. We do not want to believe there are things we must do in order to preserve life or must not do in order not to promote death. As a result, not wholly committing to preserve life on Earth, we are in danger of falling in with death—the corruption and violence that threaten life on Earth. We abdicate our responsibilities for this life and live instead like angels-in-waiting who live for the next life, or like mere animals who live day-to-day.

Does it make sense to say that deep down we want to live like gods, beings who can do whatever they want and have all their dreams come true—like live forever "knowing good and evil" (Gen 3:5)—which today means creating our own standards of good and evil? When we behave that way, the daily work of moral living—protecting and preserving life, opposing threats to it, building up others, striving to discern good from evil, acting on our commitments, being wrong, needing forgiveness from others, making amends, etc.—are burdens we prefer not to bear and so avoid. They get in the way of our pursuit of happiness. Avoiding that strife, leaving it to others, and looking past this life to some other world are all temptations we easily give in to. When that happens, we are less attentive to corruption and violence and the insidious ways they infiltrate our lives, we are less vigilant to identify and call out destructive dealings and so less prepared to oppose them. And when that happens, the future of life on Earth is even more exposed to threats and endangered by careless behavior, bringing us closer to the destruction looming over us. Wanting to be like gods, without anything over and above us—like death and standards of good and evil—we lose sight of the moral work before us. Destructiveness advances and the darkness around us deepens.

We will elaborate upon this temptation to be like gods later in this section. Before we do, we can point out how worldviews that disregard the future of life on Earth stem from our failure to apply our basic moral principle, from wishful metaphysical thinking, and from archaic religious ideas.

Everyone has entertained this idea: "Why should it matter what becomes of the world after I am gone? Why should I care about a world I will not live to see? I won't be there. The future of the world is not my reality now, and when it is I won't be there to experience it, so why be concerned about it? Besides that, today's problems are so large and complicated there is nothing I can do about them anyway. So why try? Better to live for today. Or, better to look beyond this world to the next one."

The short answer is that we ought to care about a future we will not live to see. Reflecting upon the practically universal—and certainly biblical—rule to "do to others as you want them to do to you" shows us this. The full extension of the golden rule reaches out to a future we know is coming but will not live to see and so includes those whose lives we will affect but never know. When we are able to influence the world for the better, it is up to us to do what we can to do so and so improve the lot of those who come after us.

When we start out in life, it is understandable that we take the measure of our lives by what we can do for ourselves within the span of our own lives. My life, my possessions, my rights, my accomplishments, my reputation, my career are what matter. Eventually, though, we see that it is shortsighted and immature to live that way. While we might think that it is only what we do and experience now that matters, in the big scheme—which is never out of our sight—it is our influence on the lives of others and of those who come after us that really count. The significance of our lives cannot be assessed now, either by ourselves or others now living, but only in the future, by those not yet living.

Imagine that when we die we face a moral tribunal. Call them the "golden rulers." It will be composed of representatives of future generations who must live with the effects of our actions, as well as of earlier generations who can assess how effectively we were stewards of the improvements they made to our lives. What will their judgment be? How will they assess what we have done with our lives? Given what we know about natural and human history, as well as what we can do to shape the future, it should be evident that our moral responsibilities extend to those who come after us and even to those who went before us. We can imagine what they would have us do, and we can ask, "What ought we do for future generations if their future would be our future, and what would past generations expect us to do with the improvements they made to our lives?" It is a sign of our humanity that we respect our forebears and the improvements they handed on to us and that we take responsibility for the future we leave to our descendants. They are our generational neighbors. Are we doing for the next generation what we would hope they would do for us if our places were reversed? Are we managing the resources and valuing the achievements the previous generation gave us to preserve and protect? We might consider: will they think that we failed them, that we squandered their inheritance because we were too self-absorbed or failed to see where our self-indulgence was taking the world?

"Do to others as you would have them do to you" rings true for all of us; whether or not we heed it is another matter. "Others" may refer initially to loved ones, family, friends, and neighbors, but eventually extends, in varying degrees, to fellow citizens, other human beings, fellow Earthlings, as well as to those who will come after us, even reaching back to those who went before us. From our widest historical point of view, and certainly from a theological point of view, all are our kin for whom, to greater and lesser degrees, we should have regard and are responsible. It is a sign of moral maturity to see our lives this way and to welcome the judgment of the golden rulers. As we grow up, gratitude to our forebears who strove to make the world a better place grows too; the understanding that we should do the same for those who come after us, also, is a horizon we continue to move toward. Previous generations looked out for us; we are glad they did, and we should do the same for future generations. It is to our credit, then, when we critically judge our lives from the standpoint of those who came before us and will come after us. Moral grown-ups come to see that a generation that lives only for itself, with no regard for other generations, is to be pitied. Making the world a better place for those who come after us, we come to see, is what makes life worth living. Advancing the human project and magnifying the dignity of human life is what counts, ultimately.

To reiterate, everyone has had the idea: "Why should the future of life on Earth matter when the universe is doomed?" Since the long-term future of life on Earth is bleak, why should we care what happens to it after we're gone? Whether we acquire that idea from scientific projections or Christian prophecy, it is a widespread view that the universe has no future. Scientific projections ending in a Big Freeze, Big Crunch, or Big Rip, and Christian prophecies foretelling God's destruction of the world have formed the presumption that the universe is done for. That expectation also might explain why we lose interest in the world after we are gone. It is no wonder we are not invested in the future of life on Earth when we presume that it is destined for destruction anyway.

It is important to note, in the first place, that scientific projections are not certainties. When we learn more about 95 percent of matter and energy in the universe that we suppose exists but know little about, we will better understand the universe's prospects. Furthermore, we do not know how many generations will come after us, or how far we can extend life beyond our planet, or whether there is other intelligent life that can extend life far into the future.

The uncertainty of these scientific projections, furthermore, can lead to metaphysical speculations that take our eye off of the future of life on Earth. An example of this is the idea that our universe is one of an infinite number of universes, or of a multiverse. Thinking that way can lead us to distance ourselves from the natural laws and moral rules that ground our lives in this world. Maybe there are different laws of nature in other universes; maybe there are different logics; maybe for intelligent life in other universes, the golden rule doesn't apply. And if they do not apply out "there," how can we be so sure they are true "here?" Perhaps other universes are entangled with and intermingling with our universe so that we cannot really be sure what "our" universe is, etc. Imagining an infinite number of universes, we are tempted to speculate about future lives in other worlds, slackening our decisive commitments to life in this world.

Finally, ancient Christian prophecy that God intends to destroy the world also takes our attention away from the future of life on Earth. Those "prophecies," though, do not hold up under historical investigation. When we investigate them, we realize that they were not cosmological predictions but longings of suffering people who prayed to God to stop the worldly powers that oppressed them.[4] When we realize that, the expectation that the universe is doomed drops away. Critical biblical theology, instead, can give hope that the Creator will protect the universe from destruction, preserve life on Earth, and prepare the way for the Lord's reign. It may well be that the universe will disintegrate and reduce to nothing but useless radiation; but if it does, it is baseless to claim that this was Christian prophecy.

We should care about the future of life on Earth because it makes sense to believe (being cautious with such projections, leery of wishful metaphysics, and contrary to these prophecies—but consistent with biblical theology) that the world came into being purposefully, that it is being sustained, that chaos is being restrained, and that the world has a future. It is *this* world, the world we know, not some completely new, utterly different reality discontinuous with this world, or some heavenly, spiritual world we know nothing about, that is to be saved from the darkness. Dismaying as it is to contemplate a disintegrating universe, if that is in fact what happens in the end, we can do better than simply say that this is just the way matter is or what God wills. The better explanation is that the deep darkness and formless void, present at the beginning, prevailed in the end, not that God destroyed his creation or that its disintegration is simply a brute, inscrutable fact.

It is understandable that we wonder about what happens "after our life on Earth." We speculate about our continued existence in heaven, or in some spiritual world, or in another universe. We should, though, be critical of wishful thinking that invites us to assume our continued existence somewhere else. Where earlier generations feared damnation or the grave, worrying that that was their final destination, now many happily believe in a blissful immortality, expecting to "pass on" to the "next life" where "new experiences await," and where they might be "reunited with loved ones" forever. Certainty of an afterlife, future journeys, and spiritual destinations seem to be ours for the wishing, whether or not we believe in God.

It is indeed a comforting thought that I will beat death; so, I might think, why shouldn't I believe it? For us, "all our dreams can come true." So who's to say that my desire for life after death isn't possible? If my dream of an endless future gives me comfort, why should I be denied it? Believing in God may make such a future real for me, or maybe wishing upon a star does. It seems obvious, for instance, for those who experience a personal relationship with God—who is immortal and spiritual—that they, too, are immortal, spiritual beings. Many Christians expect, evidently, that their

---

4. Biblical references to "creating a new heaven and a new Earth" or "destruction by fire" pertain not to the destruction of the natural world but to the renewal of life on Earth. The concern is more ethical than cosmological. For a helpful discussion, see chapter 4 of Wilkinson, *Christian Eschatology*. See also Westermann, *Isaiah*, 408.

relationship with God will continue without interruption after death: when they "die," they go to heaven to be with God and their loved ones. This surely looks as though they believe that they are like gods who never die. In the garden of Eden Adam and Eve seized godlike powers by eating a fruit. Now we have them simply by believing we do. We readily believe that we are like gods in that we will "not die." We do not need to be tempted by a serpent to think that way.

We are tempted by our consciousness that suggests, "You will not die." It will insist, "Death cannot stop your self-awareness; you will continue to exist in heaven, or in another universe, or in a spiritual realm of your own choosing." Beguiled by this wishful thinking, we overlook the finality of death. Enticed to look beyond this life to some future existence, we look past death and ignore the corruption and destruction that bring death nearer to us. We walk away from the fight to defend life, seduced by assurances that it's not worth the hardship, that more interesting experiences await us. In this way we leave the field—life itself—vulnerable, open to corruption and destruction. We abandon our post, we lay down the weapons that might enable us to prevail in the battle—our reason, emotions, and will—for the lure of an endless pursuit of new experiences. Preferring the wish that death won't stop my life, over the certainty that I will die, I dream of future experiences rather than prepare to confront the challenges in front of me, thereby drawing death—the corruption and violence around me—ever closer. I am so busy entertaining all the pleasant things I want to experience in this life—writing up my "bucket list" before passing on to the "next chapter of my life"—that I ignore the destruction closing in around me.

In this way we become more accepting of corruption and violence, less willing to fight off its many surrogates—oppression, abuse, hatred, spite, lies, etc.—ignoring the fact that, in our day, violence can spiral out of control and lead to the death of all life. The natural death of an individual is inevitable; the death of human civilization and of life on Earth are not. Knowing what we do about the fragility of life on Earth and the human capacity for violence, the destruction of life is a threat we must oppose if we are not to contribute to life's demise. Yet, by telling myself that death won't be the end of me—of my self-awareness and my capacity for future experiences—I weaken my resolve to bear hardships for others and console myself with the thought that, after all, they too have better things to look forward to. So why cause myself the hardships required of me to oppose death and defend life?

If I thought I would live forever, like a Greek god, nothing would have any value over anything else because at one time or another in my unending life, anything could be pleasing to me. It would be a life of unending dabbling with no real consequences, no real conclusions, no real improvements or failures. How could I tell what is better or worse from one thing or another when my life is headed to no place in particular since there is no goal to define my endless life? Given enough time, I might think I can get used to or get over any experience. It is only because of the finality of death that particular values rise before me, directing me on the path of the moral life where there are real rights and wrongs, true improvements and failures. The emergence of values follows from the way human life and death relate: without life there can be no values, obviously; but without death the value of this particular life would not become self-evident to us, nor would the importance of those attitudes, capabilities, and actions that serve to protect and give dignity to this life.

Values emerge, then, because of the way death limits human life. At the same time, we can see, values take on a life of their own, they impart meaning to life, make life worth living, give purpose to life, and are even worth dying for—*giving up* life for. We realize this when we see that dying for the right reasons dignifies human life. Ultimately, then, our lives serve values in that values like truthfulness, loving-kindness, selflessness, courage, etc.— that which gives dignity to human life—become the object of our common concern, extending beyond our individual lives. When we live with these values in view, moreover, our lives manifest or exhibit and so communicate the dignity of human life to others; and, insofar as human life is dependent upon and intertwined with all life, living this way shows forth the value of all living things. In that way the dignity of human life outlasts individual lives, extends beyond the lives of particular communities and cultures, and endures.

For angelic, godlike beings, though, who do not exist in the context of life limited by death but of unlimited existence with endless experiences—where they can choose or reject any value they wish with indifference and without final consequence—moral living is a burdensome restriction. Since, though, we are humans, beings who die and are victims to corruption and violence—but who also have the capability to protect life and oppose death—it is our place to preserve life and strive to discern good from evil: in other words, to live mortal and moral human lives, not immortal amoral lives. I can be tempted to live like a god, though, when my ultimate concern is the pursuit of happiness. Responsibility for the lives of others gets in the way of that pursuit. I prefer to live in a world without moral responsibilities because they detract from the happiness I seek. What I live for are good experiences: I plan for them, anticipate them, savor them when they happen, enjoy them all over again when I remember them, and curate and assemble them into narratives I can show and tell others—itself a pleasurable experience—and dream of future experiences in my next life.

Connected to the temptation to believe that I am like a god who will live forever is the temptation to believe that I am like a god who has knowledge of good and evil. It is common today to think that all morality is subjective, in the eye of the beholder, no one's moral standards being better than anyone else's. For us, evidently, that's what the knowledge of good and evil amounts to. When I think that good and evil are subjective, I am subject only to my own morals—which may change—so that what is "good" for me now I might judge "bad" for me later. What this means, practically, since I am the judge of my own moral behavior, is that moral standards do not apply to me. I am above all standards.

It is that thought—there are no moral standards to discover and follow—that becomes the real knowledge of good and evil. Now I don't have to work to discriminate between good and evil, searching for real differences, testing my understanding in the hope that I might improve my moral knowledge. Instead, knowing that there is no real standard for good and evil, I can choose to believe whatever I want whenever I want. From this godlike perspective I pretend to claim a higher, truer insight into good and evil. Since there is no real moral standard governing our lives that we can gain insight into, apply, fall short of, and improve upon, I can take a place above all standards, choose one I like, even create one. In this way, too, I become godlike.

This idea—real knowledge of good and evil is that there is no difference between good and evil—is godlike in that it places us above the human search for moral wisdom, allowing us to be lords over all rules, permitting us to choose the ones we prefer—like gods—or, if we choose, live with none at all—like animals. From this godlike vantage point, morality need not involve responsibility, praise, guilt, mercy, forgiveness, amendment of life—all matters of life and death—but simply preferences—mere matters of taste. We can choose to observe moral rules or not, whatever amoral beings prefer. Because the rules are our own rules, we can make them as high or low, as stringent or lax as we choose, whatever makes for the most happiness, whatever makes us feel good about ourselves. Then we can be self-assured in doing whatever we want with no regret. In these ways, we choose an easier path because it ignores basic facts that come with moral living, such as the natural limit of death and the weight of responsibility. Gods don't fret over such things, and animals don't think about them. Human beings do indeed have knowledge of good and evil; what that means for beings like us, though, is that we have to strive to discern good from evil, since we do not have godlike certainty of good and evil. Real human knowledge of good and evil—like all our knowledge—is partial, develops, and takes work to acquire.

Like Adam and Eve, then, we yield to the temptation to be like gods when we think we are not mortal but immortal, as well as when we think we are above morality or are amoral. We think we are above morality when we think we are subject only to those standards we choose for ourselves so that the only "demands" morality places on us are ones we put on ourselves. If there is a moral law "above" me, it is simply the law of self-preservation, the right to do whatever I need to do to survive, something animals naturally follow. But that, of course, only further solidifies my desire to act out of self-interest and so again places me above all moral standards, allowing self-interest to overrule them. Ultimately, I want to enjoy this life as long as I can until I "pass on" to the "other side" where new experiences await me. Even the moral rule "don't do to others what you wouldn't want them to do to you," while it may seem to be over me and place demands on me, can be twisted to reinforce the law of self-preservation: it guides me to look out for myself, to be prudent, to maximize my own opportunities, not to burn bridges I might need to get ahead, to be shrewd, etc. In this way, amorality, the law of self-preservation, is preserved; and morality, other-regard, the willingness to give of myself for others, makes no demands on me.

We can be tempted, then, to turn from our moral standing as stewards of life and caregivers for each other and choose instead easier roles, acting like gods or animals, even though we know better than to behave like that and know it will lead to destructiveness, as it did for Adam and Eve. We can be tempted to take these easier paths because the way to being good stewards of life and caregivers for one another is difficult and costly. When we allow ourselves to behave like immortal, amoral gods, not mortal, moral humans, we come to think that Earth is not our real home but only a temporary stopover for some future existence, and we think that moral rules do not place real responsibilities on our lives but only pose artificial, arbitrary restrictions. In a similar way, we abdicate moral responsibility when we convince ourselves that we are merely animals, nothing but earth—matter randomly coming together and coming apart. In these ways we are tempted, like Adam and Eve, to be something we aren't. Not humans but gods or animals.

We choose these easier paths, to summarize, when we think that death will not end our existence. When we do that, moral living—which is real only for beings whose lives face death every moment, both the death of termination and the death of corruption—becomes a secondary matter, maybe optional, and so something we do half-heartedly, or just enough to get by, or as much as we have to. Moral rules—fit for human beings threatened by death—do not apply to me because death does not apply to me. I am not bound, then, by responsibilities that come with this life because I am not bound by this life. Like a god, I am free to choose any rules I want and choose any afterlife I want. Or, when we think there really is no such thing as "good and evil," we can live without reference to them, like amoral animals free from moral constraints. Either way, I can convince myself to believe that the ramifications of my actions on Earth don't really matter. Either I die like any other animal without leaving a trace of any moral significance or I won't die but exist elsewhere in some other world, indifferent to what becomes of life on Earth.

Just as in the story of Adam and Eve, there are ramifications that stem from trying to be something we aren't. What befell Adam and Eve and their descendants was violence, ever-cascading violence, leading to the destruction of the world. Could that happen to us? Could violence spin out of control and unleash destruction that would be impossible to contain? Darkness would settle over civilization, and chaos would triumph in the end. No one wants this, though we ourselves would have brought it about, and we would have no excuse for it. Human beings would have made choices that led to their own demise. It is no explanation to say that God brought it about, or that that's just what matter came to. It is more illuminating to say that human beings chose that future. Strange as it may seem, human beings with hearts, souls, and minds make choices that corrupt life, and that lead to destruction and chaos—threatening a return to darkness. Why is this? It is because we can be tempted, as we have seen, to spurn moral, human life for godlike or animal life, thereby inviting the destruction of life. It might not be that we directly choose to be destructive—though sometimes violence attracts us and we become violent. In small ways, though, we corrupt our lives with lies, neglect, abuse, and harms that lead to resentments, animosities, and hostilities, feeding into a spiral of aggression that may be impossible to stop.

We know, given where we have come from and where we might be going, that disorder can darken life on Earth, civilization, and perhaps the universe forever. It is only wishful thinking to believe that disorder always leads to new order, or that darkness always gives way to the light of a new day, or that the passage of time always leads to progress. Sometimes disorder leads to decay, disintegration, and destruction—which we know may be final. The reason for this is that darkness is real, present at the beginning and perhaps at the end, challenging light and life, and because—strange as it may seem—sometimes we "love darkness rather than light."

But if we could believe that there is a purposeful plan active in the world to oppose the darkness, and that our lives can be part of this plan, we might live differently. We could see that we live in the middle of this clash, and could embrace our responsibilities as caretakers of the Earth. Then we would have a fighting chance against the disorder surrounding us. Even more, we would have hope for the future since we believe that we are here and have the capacities and responsibilities we do because of the working out of a purposeful plan. With that faith we might take the leap to love others in the hope that life and light will prevail over the darkness.

WHAT WE CAN'T KNOW BUT MIGHT BELIEVE

We have confidence in our knowledge of the natural world, as we noted. We believe we can understand the mechanisms that explain the way nature behaves, accurately predict when natural events will occur, the way they will, etc. What is the basis of this confidence? It rests on assumptions concerning the uniformity, regularity, and integration of the natural world that pertain to the way the world is, was, and will be. Several of those assumptions, or scientists' working convictions, are that matter behaves the same on Earth as it does light-years away, that the harmonies we observe now are consistent throughout space and time, and that the natural world is a whole of interrelated parts. Without these assumptions, scientific investigations would flounder, and they would not yield the comprehensive, fruitful knowledge they do. We have confidence in these assumptions because they have held up under scrutiny and stood the test of time. We have reason to believe they are well founded and worth following and relying on. While we cannot know that these convictions concerning the way the world is are true, we can believe they are sound.

Now we might doubt these convictions. But then we would limit our knowledge to what is local, temporary, and partial, and could not claim an understanding that is universal, abiding, and general. But if we embrace these convictions and gain this confidence, we have to consider: aren't we thereby entertaining or endorsing fundamental truths about the way the world really is? These convictions concerning the orderliness of the natural world maintain that something more than the random connection and dissolution of matter is taking place in it. This way of thinking, that is to say, contends that the natural world is comprised not simply of matter-in-motion but constituted by principles that form matter in regular, orderly, and harmonious ways. It is sensible, then, to ask whether there is a reason for this ordering or an origin for it. These orderings and organized systems in nature suggest something mindful, and the development and purposiveness of living things suggest something willful. Something understandable, we can believe, is taking place within the world as a whole. We can consider, then, that there is something meaningful or superordinate to be "read off" of these natural regularities and developments, and that there is a wider context informing what is going on the world. Something is going on here.

We might consider, then, contrary to materialism, that matter is not all there is, that the universe is not constituted simply of matter. We can imagine that, in the beginning, matter was only formless potential—standing in need of formation so that it could become a universe—and we can consider that something more was in play to form the universe. We might consider that in order to form a cosmos from a formless chaos—to give matter's potential direction and purpose—matter needed to be informed, given information, ordered by regularities and constancies or laws. It was due to these regularities and constancies providing stability over time and space that matter organized into increasingly complex structures and systems. It is reasonable to think, then, that some initiative informed matter with information to form it into an organized cosmos so that it was not a chaos—as the beginning universe was, as parts of it still are, and as it might yet become.

At the same time, as a corollary to this, it is reasonable to think that matter on its own would not disintegrate and come to nothing. It makes sense to think that something is opposing and undermining its formation, or disordering and misinforming it. We might account for this in a similar way by suggesting that there is something actively holding back and undermining matter's development. On this way of thinking, then, matter is raw potential standing in need of information so that it might actualize its potential; but it is also subject to misinformation that can arrest, confuse, misguide, and even destroy that potential. This observation—that disorder threatens to upend nature's purposiveness, even that the universe as a whole might disintegrate—suggests that destructiveness is also in play.

We might reason, then, that the ordering we observe has an origin and that it is purposive. More fully, we can comprehend how a purposeful plan could generate a cosmos from chaos, forming matter from formless energy, evolving eventually into a living world with self-conscious beings. It is because the laws that make life possible and the principles that make human life sustainable are manifestations of an originating plan that we are here, that we can understand our place in the universe, and that we can act on that knowledge. That plan stems from an initiative that aims not only to generate a cosmos from chaos but to preserve the orders that make life possible, protect life from lifelessness, and promote life that can do the same. We also see, though, that this purposeful plan is contested. We might consider, then, that the disordering we observe, threatening to return life to lifelessness, also has an origin.

We can account for our rational and moral capacities if they are the result of a mindful and purposeful plan working its way through matter. Our ability to understand our world, to empathize with others, and to act freely arise from a purposeful ordering active in the beginning, aiming to raise up beings who can protect and promote life. These capacities give us freedom to live "above" animal life and to generate moral principles.

On this way of thinking, the emergence of self-conscious beings was neither an accident nor an edict but the working out of a purposeful—though contested—plan emerging over time. The evolution of minds, hearts, and wills has an origin, and that initiative continues to be active throughout the material world and in us. It is the result, from a biblical point of view, of a life-giving wisdom that aims to free matter from a formless void so that it could develop its potential for life. This plan indicates purposefulness—mindfulness and willfulness, even empathy. This plan, though, also faces opposition. It may be overturned or not realize its goal. It may even fail because we do not use our minds, hearts, and wills, or misuse them for destructive purposes. Too often we do not exercise those capacities but live "beneath" them, choosing corruption and violence instead.

That purpose, most simply, is that a cosmos come into being. For that to happen, the chaos disordering its potential must be opposed. More fully, it is by generating the orders that make life possible, protect life from lifelessness, and promote human life—life that itself can help preserve and protect life—that the cosmos persists and chaos is opposed. Insofar as we participate in that purpose, we are part of it; insofar as we do not, we are acting at odds with it.

Now the purposiveness we see in the universe can be explained in a number of ways. Panpsychism, the idea that all matter has some form of consciousness, or pantheism, the idea that God and nature are different ways of speaking of the same reality, might provide adequate worldviews.[5] But given the history and the expected future of our universe, and in light of our moral experience, and with an eye toward the biblical worldview, we might see that there is a larger purpose in play in the universe, one characterized by the contention we have described.

There is a better explanation that accounts for matter developing from a formless void, for there being life-giving order, for intelligent, moral life, as well as for matter being subject to disintegration. In short, there is an origin for this ordering that is mindful, willful, and empathetic; there is also a disordering that kept matter bound, continues to frustrate its development,

---

5 Thomas Nagel considers panpsychism as an alternative to materialism and theism in *Mind and Cosmos*.

and that may bring about its annihilation in the end. If not for an insurgent act, which freed matter from chaos so that it could become a cosmos, there would not have been a universe, life, human existence, and no moral imperative for humans to protect, preserve, and promote life. It is a reasonable belief, then, that something purposeful is present in the ordering of the universe. Judging from where we are, that purpose was to oppose chaos and to draw out matter's potential, culminating in intelligent, moral beings, beings who themselves could protect, preserve, and promote life. It is our purpose, accordingly, to use our intelligence and moral sense to oppose the disorder that threatens to end life and to help others do the same.

The idea that the regularities and constancies helping to form our world have an origin is not an unusual idea. Biblical theology, for example, has maintained that the principled informing that forms the world is the wisdom or spirit of God active from the beginning. Biblical authors also gesture toward chaos—a real, active disordering—that undermines the world. While we can say, then, that the source of this ordering is purposeful—mindful, willful, and even empathetic—from what we have said we cannot conclude that it is omnipotent and omniscient. We would not conclude, in other words, that God is a supreme being but rather the purposeful initiative that brought the cosmos into existence and contends with chaos to sustain it.

Both the biblical and the scientific perspectives, broadly conceived, can align on this point. From the traditional biblical perspective, the Word of God guides the universe with wisdom. A scientific understanding can be congruent with this because it too affirms the orderliness of the universe and can consider that there is a reason for this or that there is an intelligent initiative present with it. Our scientific perspective, additionally, maintains that the universe evolves, indicating that it is not predetermined or entirely predictable. This understanding, that creation is continual, can be part of a contemporary biblical perspective as well.[6] A biblical view, finally, offers a way to understand the disorder in the universe, suggesting that something intransigent opposes the plan informing and giving purpose to the world.

On this way of reasoning, then, we can conceive of an originating principle or plan constituting the universe in the way a constitution forms a nation, informing matter, bringing our world into being, and providentially guiding it. In this way, we provide a reason why our world manifests the constancy and orderliness it does and consider that there is a purposeful origin for this, unlike materialism, which has no explanation for these

---

6. Many theologians and scientists advocate this. Two examples are Haught, *God After Darwin*; Miller, *Finding Darwin's God*.

things. This way of thinking, additionally, need not posit a God in the way we often conceive of God: a supreme being who can do anything or perform any miracle. That way of thinking imagines God as a volatile supernatural cause, something that has no role in our natural understanding. Because if that were the case, we could not have confidence that the natural laws informing nature were really indicators of a predictable universe. It would mean that natural events were ultimately not understandable and reliable, and that the laws informing them worth studying, learning, and observing; but that nature is indecipherable and its laws arbitrary, subject to supernatural impulses. It is more constructive to propose an originating source for those regularities—or for the information imparted to form matter constituting a world that develops into living things and rational beings—rather than suppose that there is an agent who miraculously interferes with those regularities—regularities which are, after all, the very bases for our ability to understand anything at all in the world. This is the idea of God we come to when we reflect on our confidence in our knowledge of the world, as well as the imperative to help preserve it from destruction, in contrast to theism, which explains away the disordering powers in the world.

In short, "God" does not name a supreme being or identify an actor in heaven. God, rather, designates the origin of the principles that inform nature, order natural life, give our lives purpose, and direct the universe. Thinking in terms of originating principles or a constituting plan, we can conceive of an origin, understand its implementation, and imagine a goal. We have seen, however, that this goal is opposed. Besides this ordering there is also disordering. Besides informing there is misinforming. There is chaos from the beginning that contests this goal and confuses its implementation, challenging the world's purpose, and that may reign supreme in the end.

Now to assert that the orderliness of the universe stems from originating principles and that its purposiveness comes from a constituting plan is anthropomorphic to a point because it projects something like our own intelligence and intentions onto the foundation and formation of the universe. But it does not do so in a small-minded way. Scientists, it is instructive to note, realize that they cannot simply project their ideas of order onto the world, because their ideas are often wrong. They need, it is more accurate to say, to discover them there. Theologians, similarly, know the dangers of creating God in their own image, and a biblical perspective limits our capacity to comprehend God. Both, finally, realize that while our understanding is improving, the nature and destiny of the universe surpass our understanding, and that there can be a place for thoughtful faith: beliefs that guide our actions so that they accord with the way we know the world to be and that ground our hope.

For the same reason, it is mistaken to attribute the destructive disordering we observe to a person, like a devil, and misleading to think of it as an evil spiritual power. Such ideas do not connect with our contemporary understanding. We are also led astray if we imagine an equal and opposite counterpart to God, as in dualism. There are more constructive ways to conceive of the diabolical reality we observe and that the biblical authors pointed to. We might more pertinently imagine something that confuses and obstructs natural development and human life. Today, for example, we are aware of the way mis- and disinformation disrupts cells and organisms, the way deception and lies can destroy human relationships, and the way malware and malicious viruses can infect and paralyze information systems. That may be a more useful way to imagine chaotic activity in the world. The chaos we envision is not evil, in the way traditionally thought, but diabolical: less demonic than corrupting, less terrorizing than entrapping, less murderous than lifeless, less cataclysmic than insidious—though the final result of such disordering can be a return to nothingness.

To develop this perspective, then, we need to reimagine the way we traditionally understand God's activity in the world as well as the opposition to it. The storylike account in the Bible of a heavenly king who intervenes in the world to affect specific changes conflicts with our understanding of natural and historical events. Today, we understand that the world is ordered by continuing laws and consistent patterns, not controlled by divine or demonic agents unpredictably intervening in it. It is no longer constructive to think of God as a supreme being, or, in the anthropomorphic terms of the Bible, as an actor in nature or history. That view is at odds with our understanding of natural occurrences as well as our understanding of the course of human affairs. Our confidence in natural law, rather, affirms the constancy and orderliness of the natural world, as does our conviction that there are moral rules that govern human life and human patterns that organize it. A view based upon episodic interventions by supernatural agents undermines our current understanding. If we held such a view, we would undercut our practice of experimenting and making predictions; consequently we would question our confidence that we can change the world for the better, and weaken our resolve to do so. Instead, we would be enticed to appeal to supernatural powers to influence the course of nature and human events.

Today we assume that there are laws governing nature and rules ordering human life so that we can generalize, project, and predict, and consequently make decisions in the world with confidence. If we think, though, that God is a supreme being who intervenes in the world and performs miracles, suspending natural laws and upending historical patterns, we would act differently. We would think that by petitioning God in prayer, practicing rituals, or performing good deeds we could persuade God to alter the course of natural, human, and personal affairs. There may well be a kind of empowerment in these religious actions, but it is not the kind that directly alters the course of nature and history. If we truly believed that, we would spend more time praying and performing religious rituals, hoping that God would directly alter the course of events, instead of painstakingly learning natural laws, constructing moral rules, and understanding historical patterns so that we ourselves could shape the course of events.

In earlier times religious people could do little more than call upon God to change the world, piously accepting whatever happened in the world. That is no longer the case. Such piety and actions, moreover, do not strengthen hope and love but lead to a more passive role for creatures in the creation, less interested in stewarding God's creation, more concerned with finding solace in the world or escaping it altogether. We now live in a time when we have the means to intervene in the world for better, as well as meddle in it for worse. Too often, though, we turn a blind eye to the fate of the world and simply pursue our own happiness, now or in the hereafter. We are equipped better than any previous generation to improve the world and to restrain the chaos menacing our world; our indifference to doing so, however, and our fixation with ourselves only strengthen it.

The theological thinking proposed maintains that we would be better stewards of the creation by devoting our time and energy to learn nature's ways, history's patterns, and human tendencies than petitioning God to change them. It would be better to have faith that there is an originating initiative that ordered our world, that it is active in nature, and that it is continually working through the regularities and patterns we have come to understand—and then to act on that faith by using our capacities to engage with those regularities and patterns—than to appeal to God to interfere with them. Rather than be supplicants, we should be actors who use our time and effort to utilize the capacities generated in us—our reason, our emotions, and our wills—to understand the laws governing nature and to follow the rules guiding human life. Faith is not "turning your life over to God" or "letting God take over" if that means abandoning those capacities or abdicating one's responsibilities. To have faith, rather, is to take charge of our capacities and to engage with those established orders. Otherwise, "trusting in God" comes to mean discounting our capabilities and discrediting our agency. To "let God be praised" or to act "to the glory of God," instead, is to stir up our abilities and lift up our actions so that they become conduits for creative and life-giving activity in a world threatened with destruction.

Faith does not wait. Faith does not wait for divine intervention. Faith acts. Faith acts knowing it has capabilities to oppose lifelessness and to protect life—knowing as well that inaction strengthens lifelessness. Faith uses prayer and religious practices to strengthen itself for that work, but it does not presume it can cause the divine to do that work. Faith grasps what is going on in the world and how it can improve the world, but it does not presume to know what is going on in heaven or how heaven intercedes in the world. Faith does not believe the unbelievable; it does not resort to miracles or to the merely possible in order to explain what happens in the world. It looks, rather, to natural potential and regularities to explain what is most plausible. Faith does not test one's credulity. It proves itself, rather, by engaging with realities actually at play in the world. It is no credit to faith to believe the incredible, or to expect the implausible, or to wait for heaven to act. Genuine faith stands upon what it knows to be true about the world and acts on that, not on its willingness to believe what does not seem true or to wait for miracles to happen.

At this point we have to ask: "But isn't that the idea of God, God's actions in the world, and faith held by most believers today?" God is the Creator of the world, to whom you can pray with the certainty that he can enter into and change the course of your life, which means that if God wills, God can even intervene in the course of natural events. In reply, we have to ask: "Doesn't such a belief actually enfeeble God's work in the world?" It does if we do not fully utilize our capacities, take charge of our responsibilities, and fail to engage with the regularities God has established.

In our time, it is true, "God" almost always conjures up the idea of a heavenly Father, the King of the universe, or the Big Guy Upstairs who decides to intervene—or not—in the world. The belief that God is a supernatural actor who miraculously intervenes in nature and history, however, gets in the way of articulating a theological understanding for our world today. Because in that case, typically, the real motive for believing in God is to have a relationship with a heavenly Father who will enter into your life to protect you, help solve your problems, and comfort you now and in all eternity. This commonly held belief, though, is detrimental not only to our understanding of what is going on in nature and history but to our personal lives as well. It puts in motion a way of thinking that leads away from the thoughtful faith that a purposeful plan informs and guides nature and history, misleading us into thinking that God is a miracle-worker, tempting us to use God as a means to our own ends, and so departs from the path of genuine faith, hope, and love. Consequently, it will not encourage us to develop our intelligence, compassion, and willpower, or the capacities we need to fortify ourselves against corruption and destruction. It will not, finally, inspire genuine love and hope because, instead of working to preserve and prosper our world, it encourages us to live for another. Such a way of thinking can even—given the destruction active in our world—aid corruption and violence.

Biblical faith should be congruent with a truthful understanding of what is really going on in the world—a world we have seen, where chaos is real, active, and life-threatening. Biblical theology can ground and enrich our understanding of nature and history, as well as encourage us actively to engage in our world, when we start with the faith that a purposeful plan is active in the world, opposing the chaos that would destroy it. Such faith, in turn, generates hope for the future and inspires the love of others. In contrast to much religious thinking, it chooses truth over comfort, humanity's destiny over my own future, and sustaining life on Earth over passing through it en route to heaven. In that way, biblical faith employs our intelligence, willpower, and compassion—mind, soul, and heart—so that we can act in faith, hope, and love, living as good stewards on Earth.

Believers today should ask themselves whether they hold their beliefs principally because they promise a happier life now and in heaven. (And they might note that in an earlier day, one of the marks of the Christian life was suffering, not happiness.) Biblical faith does promise a "peace that passes all understanding," but that is not what the world means by "happiness," as we will see. Such peace comes not from avoiding evils in the world or from having pleasant experiences and living comfortably. It does not come, we might say, from walking away from the battle, celebrating victory, and enjoying "peace," but from fighting the good fight, believing that "God himself fights by our side"[7]—even if that does not make us happy.

A religious belief that encourages us to call upon supernatural powers to intervene in the world to protect us and to bring us happiness starts to look more like magic than faith, in that it encourages us to think that we can conjure up God's powers to act in the world. It tempts us to use God as a means to attain our own ends, turning the faithful into flatterers and stewards of the creation into pursuers of creaturely comforts. We have to ask: if our ultimate goal is happiness, in this life and in another, and if we appeal to God to obtain it, doesn't God become primarily a means to that end? God becomes the agent we appeal to who can deliver happiness, and confessions, rituals, prayers, and obedient conduct become the crafts we practice to obtain it. We misconceive biblical faith if we think that happiness is its goal, that God is the agent who intervenes in our lives to help us reach it, and that prayer and other acts of devotion are the currency we spend to gain God's favor to attain it. When believers think that such behavior

---

7. Luther, "Mighty Fortress."

demonstrates trust in his will and belief in his power, and so will gain his favor, belief begins to look like a self-serving transaction.

Ultimately, biblical faith is indeed a consolation that brings a peace passing all understanding. But it does so because it gives a truthful account of reality and the purpose of human life. Such faith inspires us to live responsibly in this world and not simply to wish for another. Biblical faith realizes, given the realities we face, that happiness or mere self-preservation cannot be the goal of life because those aims actually play into the corruption and destruction of life. It is rather love that faces up to the world as it really is and gives us hope for realizing the purposes of life. Because the darkness is real, the goal of our lives must not be the pursuit of happiness or mere self-preservation; if they are, eventually jealousy, envy, animosity, hostility, conflict, corruption, and violence will be the result. Because the darkness is real, we will see these pursuits for what they are: denial, the desire to flee from this reality, to escape it, to retreat to our bunkers, and to wish for another reality and another life.

PART TWO

PART TWO

II

What Ought We Do?

PURSUE HAPPINESS

We know that the world is poised for destruction, in the short, medium, and long terms. We do not know, though, whether "the end is at hand." With that in view, what should we do? Make the most of life while we can? "Eat, drink, and be merry, for tomorrow we die?" Prepare ourselves for the "next world?"

We should not give up on humanity, life on Earth, or the universe, for that matter. It is our place as human beings to protect life, and, as far as we can, to promote its continuance. We would not be motivated to do that, however, if we believed that the material world was done for, or if we believed that God was planning to destroy the world. Even though life's future looks bleak, we should strive to sustain it. We would be renouncing our place in the universe if we did anything less. To do that, we need a worldview that explains our place in the universe, that shows why we should live morally principled lives, and that gives us hope.

The aim of this essay is to set out such a worldview. One of the main components of that worldview, as we have noted, is the golden rule. The principle that we should do for others as we would have them do for ourselves, we will see, accords with what we know to be true about the world and what we might hope for our world. The golden rule is not meant for an ideal world or a heavenly world, and it is not targeting the gullible or chumps; it is an imperative for everyone in *this* world. The reason, as we have suggested, is just because ours is a corrupt and violent world. Without the respect for life that the golden rule impresses upon us, destructiveness could overwhelm us. That is why it is imperative for us to follow the golden rule: it preserves life, protects human beings, and promotes the dignity of human life. That is the reason the golden rule has been esteemed throughout history.

If that is the answer to the question "How should we live?," we can see that neither materialism nor theism set us on that moral path. Materialism, as we have noted, does not regard humans as free, responsible beings—any more than animals are—and so is *a*moral. Theism regards humans as angels-in-waiting and so is not rooted in this life or grounded in morality fit for *mortal* human beings. Given what we know about the threats we face today, and knowing that not following the moral path allows these threats to expand—making life worse for us and for our descendants—following a morally principled life is how we should live. That path also brings the biblical perspective into view, providing a context for love and hope. The question is whether we have the courage to live according to that worldview.

Even so, observing the way people actually live, it is easy to form the impression that, while we profess commitment to morally principled lives, in practice we are more concerned to pursue happiness or simply to preserve our own lives. And we should acknowledge, given the awareness that the future of the world looks bleak, that those seem to be sensible answers to the question "How should we live?" What should we do, given what we know about the ominous threats the world faces? In light of these threats, we might conclude that there is little individuals can do to thwart them; and, for those who only subsist or who live on the margins of society, there may well be little they can do. But for those of us who have the opportunity and means to do something, our inaction allows these threats to expand, making life worse for everyone, including our descendants. Still, if a deep darkness is the source of these threats, as this essay is arguing, isn't resistance futile? Besides, it is probably a long time before the curtain comes down on us, so why not pursue happiness as long as we can?

To begin with, "How *should* we live?" is a vital question for us to ask en route to establishing a worldview. We cannot simply dismiss it and all moral questions by answering "It's all relative" or "It's all subjective." Those are not answers at all but refusals to engage in moral inquiry, dismissing it as a matter of taste or conformity, discounting the moral insights and improvements we have made over the centuries. It is discouraging to see how often people discredit moral deliberation in this way. We should not, however, be deterred by them any more than we are by those who dismiss the question

"What can we know?," saying that scientists "don't really know anything" or that science is "only a theory." Our understanding of both our natural and moral worlds has improved and is improving.

"What should we do?" is an important moral question, and it has real answers. This means that it is a question *we* deliberate over and *act* upon. The question, that is to say, is not "What do *I want* to do?" or "What are *we compelled* to do?" It concerns neither individual desires for happiness nor animal instincts, principally, but common decisions and actions. If the question concerned individual desires, there could be no general answer: individuals would simply follow their desires for happiness. If the question concerned animal instincts, there could be no deliberating at all: we would simply be determined by nature to behave in preset ways to preserve our lives. Neither of these pertain to this moral question.

Nevertheless, these do appear to be prudent responses to our question, given the threats to our lives. As we have noted, you would have support for these views if you believed that all there is is matter in random motion. Plus, if you had the material resources, skills, and opportunities—and played your cards right—chances are that you will have a comfortable life. You needn't worry about the end of the world. Or, if you believed that this life was preliminary to another, future life, you would make the most of this life while you were here, using it to enhance your spiritual journey. So we can understand why the two most common answers to the question "What should we do?" or "How should we live?" are "pursue happiness" and "preserve your life"—even though both make the mistakes described above. What follows attempts to show the inadequacy of these viewpoints, explaining why these two answers fail to face this question with the seriousness it deserves. Then we will make the case that the right answer is "Do unto others as you would have them do to you."

The two most common, seemingly obvious answers to our question, then, are "pursue happiness" and "preserve your life." What's wrong with those answers? In the first place, lives devoted to the pursuit of happiness and to self-preservation are self-defeating and self-refuting. We can see how, on their own terms, lives driven by the pursuit of happiness or motivated by self-preservation lead to dead ends. Secondly, the consequences of following them contribute to the corruption of the world and to the disorder threatening life.

Many would answer the question "How should we live?' with "pursue happiness." That surely describes what many people strive for. For citizens of the United States, the "pursuit of happiness" seems to be a birthright, something they are entitled to. We take it for granted that happiness is what life is all about. For those who live securely and comfortably in the United States, moreover, it is easy to think that happiness is within their reach. Listening to many Christians in the United States, to compound matters, *God* wants them to be happy, in this life and in the next.[1]

We lose our way, however, when happiness, whether in this life or another, is the ultimate goal. The reason for this is that the pursuit of happiness aims at an inherently deceptive destination, what sages from around the world and throughout history have referred to as the "hedonistic paradox." The paradox is that the more we seek happiness, the more our desires and expectations grow and the further that goal recedes from us. Since our desires are never satisfied, happiness is something we never reach. We will not find happiness by chasing it; it is truer to say that a fulfilling life will "find us" when we pursue not our own happiness but rather goals that have intrinsic value.

The unending pursuit of happiness, to elaborate, makes us captive to our desires, disordering our souls. When we give our lives over to the pursuit of happiness, wishes become desires, desires become wants, wants become needs, and our sense of moderation, balance, and impartiality slips away. The pursuit of happiness numbs our mind's capacity to discern reality from fantasy, diverts our moral sensibilities from the needs of others, and saps our will to respond to them. When we do not develop our moral senses—being too intent on following our bodily senses—we weaken our capacity to see the needs of others, to empathize with them, to respond them, and to help them—all signs of a disordered soul. It becomes normal, then, for affluent and secure United States citizens like me not to hear the sounds of those in need. Long after my needs are met, my wants, desires, wishes, and whims make so much noise that they drown out the needs of others. I am out of tune with them and even lose the sensitivity to hear them.

We see an example of how this works in our personal relationships. When dire needs go unmet and unfairness is ignored, resentments and animosities build, often becoming overwhelming. We have all seen the way needs fester and burn in the souls of those afflicted, building resentment and animosity toward those who could help but do not. Correspondingly, the souls of those who could help but do not are hardened, their disregard for the needs of others dulling their moral sensibilities. This allows corruption and violence to grow and, given our capacity for destructiveness, to spin out of control, ruining relationships and communities.

The pursuit of happiness is a perilous path, moreover, because we have divergent and often conflicting views of what will make us happy so that, inevitably, we live at cross-purposes with others. This problem is amplified

---

1. According to Jeffrey Rosen, what the founders of the United States meant by the "pursuit of happiness" was not the pursuit of good feeling or pleasure but the quest for good character. *Pursuit of Happiness*, 1–15.

because we live in a world where we come into conflict over the limited material resources and opportunities needed to be happy. It is naïve, therefore, to think that this is a peaceful path all will amicably pursue. Whatever our dreams for happiness might be, there are not enough resources in the world for everyone to satisfy those dreams. The resources and opportunities required to attain happiness will always bring us into competition with others. Sometimes that competition is cooperative, but it can easily lead to hostility and conflict.

In pursuing my own happiness and seeking to gain advantages in my quest to do so, then, I am not acting from moral principle, promoting our common humanity, but competing for an edge over others. Sometimes my efforts to better my own life also betters the lives of others, but often that is not the case. A moral sense of equity, impartiality, empathy, and self-control, though, could deter me from engaging in this conflict, providing me with the willpower to temper my own desires. They may fail me, though, if I have given myself over to the pursuit of happiness. When I engage in that pursuit, competitive antagonisms too easily take over.

While seeming innocuous, then, the pursuit of happiness is inherently self-defeating and leads to unavoidable competition and conflict. The inadequacy of that answer is also borne out in our personal lives. Early in life the pursuit of happiness appears to be the goal we strive for. But as we mature, we realize that happiness constantly recedes like a mirage so that it cannot be a measure of a life well lived. Looking back at our lives, a better measure is what we have done for others, or how we have responded to and helped them. This insight comes with the realization that happiness, or, better, deep satisfaction with a life well lived, comes to us as a by-product of pursuing goals that have value in themselves—such as preserving life, protecting others, and promoting the dignity of human life—not when happiness itself is the goal of our lives.

PRESERVE YOUR LIFE

Another common response to the question "What should we do?" purports to be based on what is really going on in the world, namely "the struggle to survive." If it is true that ultimately all living things are in competition to preserve their lives, then that's what is really going on in our lives, too. In that case we can't help but live that way since all living things are hardwired to. In the popular mind, the natural and social sciences themselves (biology and economics are examples) tell us that the world is a place where only the fittest survive, where all living things are inherently selfish, and so all are in competition for the materials needed to live. Our lives, consequently, can't help but be determined by the struggle to survive. Popular thinking goes something like this: all living things compete to survive; human beings are living things; therefore, all humans compete to survive.

If that were the case, the law of self-preservation, "do for yourself first . . ." conflicts with the golden rule, "do unto others . . ." Then the moral *rule* supposedly directing how humans *should* live would conflict with natural *laws* that govern life, or with how we *actually* live, which, in biology, is the law of self-preservation, or, in economics, the law that everyone acts out of their own self-interest. If the result of following the golden rule is that you are disadvantaged or abused (at a minimum) or (at worst) marginalized or eliminated, then it looks as though our *should* conflicts with what *is*. We might think that the way we supposedly *should* live does not align with the way the world *really* is. Would that mean that the morally principled life is out of step with reality? For life in the real world, we might conclude, the golden rule simply isn't true, and we shouldn't be obliged to observe it.

So we might be tempted to think that the world is governed by "do for yourself first," not "do unto others . . ." One solution to this apparent conflict—between what we know to be true and what we ought to do—would be to treat the golden rule as a guideline, something we *might* follow but not as an imperative we are supposed to heed. We might conclude that while it *seems* to be an imperative, do unto others . . . really isn't: it is only optative, you might . . . If that is the case, then the natural law of self-preservation overrides the golden rule of other-regard, the law trumps the rule, and we follow the rule only when it suits us.

That, though, is not a solution at all but a submission. When following the golden rule has become optional—appropriate to follow with family and friends perhaps—but not imperative for life in the real world, self-preservation has canceled other-regard. The golden rule becomes an otherworldly ideal, fit for saints perhaps but not suited for those who live in the real world, not a rule for how we all should live.

Notice, furthermore, what happens when the golden rule becomes an option, not an imperative, something I follow when it suits me, or if others do, or if they go first. Then I am not following the golden rule at all; self-interest rules instead. When I calculate whether following the golden rule will benefit me, I nullify the rule's imperative to *do*, to *act for others*, to *take the initiative*—just because it's the right thing to do, just because the rule is true, not whether it benefits me. Then the formula "What's in it for me?" rules our lives, not the imperative to act for others as we would have them do for us. Instead of being inspired to think impartially, be empathetic, and act freely—engaging those moral capabilities that make us attuned to the golden rule—we are caught up in self-preservation, captive to self-interest, and unable to escape the pull of self-love. Consequently, we hesitate to follow the golden rule, hedge when we do, oftentimes simply appear to, deceive ourselves into thinking we do, and even rationalize that we shouldn't have to. As a result, we do not live by the rule we know to be true for human life, and so do not fulfill our moral capabilities or live up to our full humanity, but we allow self-preservation to govern our lives instead.

Suppose, though, we believed it was really true that everyone was only out for themselves and that we had no choice but to do the same. If I believed that everyone was striving to gain an advantage over others, I would have to think that they would also use *me* to their advantage. They would make a deal—and break it—whenever it benefited them, or whenever they could get away with it, or could fool me. On those occasions when aiding those in need would benefit them, they might do so; when, though, looking out for others disadvantaged them, drained their resources, or cost them, they would be quick to stop. So much more, then, if opposing corruption or defending others were to threaten or harm their own security, they would avoid those in distress. They might even take advantage of others' misfortune if they stood to gain by it.

Furthermore, if I believed everyone was engaged in this struggle, I would be wise to use all the means at my disposal to gain an advantage, including moral principles. I would encourage *others* to be moral—to look out for me, cooperate with me, share with me, and care for me; I would even publicly voice my commitment to "follow the golden rule"—but I would do so only when it benefitted me. Given the world we live in, it might be better to *appear* to follow the golden rule—and have the approval of others—than really do so. It is in my interest if *others* are moral; but I would not trade places with them. It would be to my advantage, actually, to lead a duplicitous life: appearing to be a moral person when that would gain the approval of others while actually pursuing what is in my own interest when no one is looking.

Finally, if I really believed that everyone was out for themselves, would I want others to know this truth about human beings? Would I *publicly* proclaim this "truth" to others that that is what is really going on in the world? No. A moment's glance shows that I would *not* want to reveal my belief to others because doing so would hinder my efforts to advance my own interests. If others knew I believed that, and that I was always plotting my own advantage, they would be suspicious of me, would not trust me, and would never enter into agreements with me—all things that would hinder my ability to advance my own interests. It is a "truth," we can see, I would keep to myself and not let others in on since I profit from living that way as long as others don't; it is not a truth everyone should heed, or a universal truth. This shows how "self-preservation is my worldview" refutes itself: if I act on it, I expose my moral duplicity—and if I am caught at it, my hypocrisy. It is a worldview arising from a disordered soul.

I would lead a double-life: I would not let others know that I do what is in my self-interest first and follow the golden rule second, or only when it suits me. I would never announce to the world, "I do not follow the golden rule but only do what's good for me," because that would put me at a disadvantage since others would be wary of me. They would be on their guard against me and not trust me, making my life more difficult.

At the beginning of this section we noted the popular belief that the sciences have determined that the world is governed by the struggle to survive. But that does not describe what is really going on in the world, and it does not describe what is really going on in our lives. It is, rather, a selective generalization, one that discounts the many cases of cooperative actions in the world. More to the point at hand, few of us are so needy that we are in life-or-death competition for the necessities required to survive. We live in stable, cooperative societies that spare most of us from such brutish struggles. For us, consequently, the slogan "Survival of the fittest is the way of the world!" does not give a truthful answer to the question "How should we live?" It is more likely a rationalization to justify our efforts to gain an advantage over others, or an excuse to avoid living morally principled lives. It may be true that ruthless behavior got us where we are, but that is no reason to continue it. Realizing that, in fact, makes it evident that it was wrong to behave that way then, and that it is wrong to do so now.

We have also noted that many suppose, wrongly, that the sciences are based on a materialistic worldview. The view that the universe consists simply of matter randomly coming together and coming apart, rather, is a *metaphysical* view, distinct from the sciences. The sciences do not rest on that worldview. Now if we thought, to spell this out, that life was simply the result of fortunate accidents of matter-in-motion, our lives would have no intrinsic purpose. Any purpose we had for our lives we would create for ourselves: we are all making up our purposes as we go along—and we would all be aware that we are all doing this. No one would believe there was a natural purpose, shared values, or a common moral principle to which our lives could better and better conform. If anyone claimed that "we should all live according to common moral principles," I would think that they were deceiving themselves, and if they tried to convince me of that, that they were attempting to deceive me. I would have to think that because, since there are no objective standards or common values or rules of conduct by which we all should live, everyone just comes up with their own standards to suit themselves—unless they were foolish enough to abide by the "objective" standards others gave them. Everyone would be out for themselves, keeping only to their own shifting, opportunistic purposes and values. It is easy to see that that would only add to the conflict and strife in the world.

Metaphysical materialism would not steel our resolve to face a world where corruption and destruction threaten to undo us. Such a worldview would not ground a way of life with the courage to challenge a violent world. It would make matters worse because it withdraws from the challenge. Why would I oppose harms done in the world if doing so would not directly benefit me or would harm me? I would avoid them—especially if it would cost me or deplete my material resources. So much more, then, I would not expend myself to oppose corruption and violence and to help others—not those present, and certainly not those living in places or in a time I will never see. I would ignore and avoid the dark things in life because they take me away from the drive to preserve my own life, and because, finally, I would not believe there is anything I can do to stop matter's inexorable descent into chaos.

The mistake in this way of thinking is to believe that we are just animals with big brains and sophisticated senses struggling to survive or be happy. We know better. This mistake overlooks those capacities that make us human beings. How could we ever discount the very capacities that allow us to wonder about these things and to ponder our worldview, to consider what we can know, what we should do, and what we can hope for? More than that, we are able to understand our world and to intervene in it; and we can help sustain life, rather than diminish it. Most especially, we have the ability to understand and empathize with others so that we can help them and make their lives better, rather than take advantage of them or harm them. That is what those capacities are for and what there is for us to do.

The lives of beings with minds, hearts, and wills—with the capacities for deliberating, apprehending, and acting—are plainly purposeful. It is reasonable to think that our purpose in life pertains to those capacities that are special if not unique to human beings and that enable humans to ask, answer, and act upon the question "What is the purpose of life?" For us, then, the answer must be more than "self-preservation" or the "pursuit of happiness" because such endeavors do not fully engage those capacities but pertain mostly to our bodily needs. Our purpose ought to engage those particular capacities and actualize their potential: to find out what's really going on in the world, to discern how others are doing, and to respond accordingly. If we do not cultivate them but allow our wishes and desires to get the better of us, we will lack the vision to see the needs of others and to perceive inequities. Worst of all, when we need minds, hearts, and wills to respond to corruption and violence, they will not be there to answer the call.

FOLLOW MORAL RULES

Picking up where we were in Part One, it is reasonable to believe that a purposeful ordering of energy and matter led to human life. This purposiveness, however, is contested; unceasing disordering is a fact of life too. In that case, how should we live, and what can we hope for?

Given who we are—self-conscious beings with minds, hearts, and wills able not simply to standpat and preserve themselves or fall back on the pursuit of happiness—the way to realize our purpose is to utilize those capacities to protect life and provide for others, giving living things the regard they are due and human beings—who have those capacities—the respect they deserve. That would fitly employ our reason, emotions, and wills, live up to our potential, and realize our purpose. If we do not, these capacities will wither up, allowing our impulses to get the better of us; if we do not, we can find ourselves, and everyone around us, on the way to tolerating deceit, falsehoods, and lies, condoning inequities and ignoring corruption, resulting in a more and more corrupt and violent world. If we do not tend to our capacities to protect life and provide for others, giving life the regard it is due and human beings the respect they deserve, we will contribute to the disorder in our social, personal, and natural worlds, and we will find ourselves living in an increasingly destructive world.

Looking back at the initial chaotic state of energy to the development of living things and finally to human beings—who are able to protect living things and one another from chaotic destruction—we can see that this is a trajectory or purpose that matches our own. From the biblical perspective, this is the goal initiated in the creation of the world from chaos; it is the path that turns away from the wide way that leads to destruction onto the narrow, hard path that leads to life (Matt 7:13); and it is the way to fulfill our role as stewards of the creation. As far as we can see, following that path is the way to fulfill our purpose in life.

This is the moral path on which humans naturally find themselves. Following it, though, leads through dark valleys. We will ask ourselves whether it is worth the risk and the cost; whether, even if we start on that path, we will make it through; whether, finally, there is light at the end of it. We know from the start that not everyone on this path will follow the golden rule but will follow, rather, other self-serving rules, such as, "Do it to others before they do it to you," "Whoever has the gold rules," or "Look out for number one." Following the difficult, narrow path, consequently, can look not only dangerous but foolish and self-defeating.

Because it is true that corruption and violence can escalate and destroy human life, as we discussed above, there are several ways we know we should *not* live if we are to prevent this. We know better, that is to say, than to add to the corruption and violence that harm others. We have codified this common knowledge in the "silver rule": do not do to others what you do not want them to do to you. This rule has been endorsed throughout history and is virtually universal. It is not hard to see why it serves as a fundamental moral principle (even if it is not followed in practice). For one, our reason immediately sees that it is a balanced equation. There is a basic equivalence in this rule, or interchangeable standard, and so strikes us as intrinsically reasonable. Second, our emotions readily imagine reversed roles, or can recognize when the "shoe is on the other foot," and so empathize with others. Finally, we realize that it is within our willpower to follow or not to follow that rule and so have responsibility for our action or inaction.

It is common moral sense, then, that there are things we should *not* do, such as cause harm to others. Following that rule keeps us from adding to the hurt and hostility in the world; but it does not actively oppose them, it will not turn back the corruption and violence in the world or stop it. While this rule points us in the right direction, then, in that it aims toward the regard living things are due and the respect human beings deserve, it does not actively oppose destructiveness; it does not confront corruption and violence.

To spell this out further, this rule places us on a path that starts in childhood and leads into moral maturity. "*Do not* do to others what you do not want them to do to you" makes sense to the reason of seven-year-olds, and we expect them to follow it: "How would you like it if they did that to you? So don't do it to them." We take it for granted that everyone has the basic moral sense to understand this rule and feels obliged to follow it. Young adults, to continue, mature when they sense the pull of the golden rule, "*do to others*": "How do you think they must feel? What can you do for them?" Adults, finally, discern the needs and concerns of others, the challenges and threats they face, and empathize with them; they cannot simply ignore them but feel the need to reach out to them in the way that they would like to be helped. We might call this the "platinum rule": "Do to others *as they would have you do* to them."

There are things I should *not* do; a corollary is that there are things I *should* do. The "silver rule" in other words, "*do not* do," evokes the "golden rule," "*Do* to others as you would have them do to you." The golden rule, in turn, evolves into the "platinum" rule, "Do to others *as they would have you do* to them," which leads us to help others in the way they would like to be helped. In this way, our natural moral capacities lead us to take steps that prompt us not only actively to oppose the harm threatening humans and other living things, but to come to their aid and help them, showing others the respect we have for ourselves. To put it differently, if I do not harm others—if I do not lie, cheat, or steal, etc.—I will be following the letter of the moral rule but not its spirit. Since the threat to human life is so real, moreover, and because corruption and violence expands and spreads, it is imperative that we oppose those threats. If we don't, we ourselves may become ensnared in destructiveness.

Following the letter of the rule might suffice for our moral purposes if the means to live dignified lives were readily available to all and our lives were not under threat. But that is not our world. There are great disparities and inequalities in our world that inevitably create resentment and animosity. All of our lives are threatened, directly or indirectly, by the conflicts this leads to. Not even the affluent can secure themselves from it. More than that, environmental calamity, cataclysmic world war, and technological disasters lie in wait for us if we do not act to stop them. It is a naïve worldview that doesn't see these threats, that doesn't see how much others are being harmed, that doesn't see how much some take pleasure in harming others, and that doesn't see how much we contribute to that harm.

Because that is the way our world is, if we fail to enter the moral path that starts with "do not do . . .," we may find ourselves on one that starts, as we discussed above, with the demand to preserve ourselves but that escalates into the desire for greater and greater security and for more and more power to maintain it. Similarly, following the pursuit of happiness accelerates into the desire for more and more comforts and pleasures and becomes servant to self-serving interests. This self-serving path increasingly leads to indifference toward our fellow travelers, to competition and to conflict, and does nothing to curtail the inevitable spread of animosities. In a world with greater and greater means for destruction in the hands of fewer and fewer people, the chance for catastrophic conflict increases. When we follow the moral path, though, respecting the dignity of others, we will not abandon them to such conflicts or surrender them to such threats but oppose them. But when we fail to see our neighbors as subjects worthy of respect, we may come to view them simply as objects in the way of our self-preservation or of our pursuit of happiness, then as adversaries that oppose us, before eventually dismissing them as things in our way—or don't even see them at all.[2]

In this volatile world, therefore, the silver, golden, and platinum rules line up with the way our world really is. In a world where corruption, violence, and destructiveness escalate and threaten all life, these moral rules, likewise, expand, amplifying the call to oppose them. If our respect for others does not increase to include active concern for them, leading us to give

---

2. For the importance of the concept of dignity and showing respect towards others, see Rosen, *Dignity*, 142–60. Another important interpreter of Kant's moral philosophy is Ronald M. Green. See "Christian Love," 261–80.

help unselfishly to others in need, these threats will pursue us and may well capture us. Destructiveness may not overwhelm us today, but it will menace others before the day is done—and maybe ourselves tomorrow.

It is not, then, merely that we fall short of making the world a better place when we don't follow these moral rules, but that we are making the world a worse place when we don't. Not pursuing the golden rule is not a neutral, innocuous option but an omission that allows our world to deteriorate; it does not leave things as they are, but it allows things to become worse. Ultimately, it is moral living that will lead to the continuation and fulfillment of life. Without it, the world will decline back into the chaos from which it came.

To summarize, many—if not most people—from all walks of life, holding a variety of worldviews, including different religious beliefs, will affirm that the answer to the question "How should we live?" is "Do unto others as you would have them do to you." The golden rule strikes all people as reasonable, even self-evident; we know, furthermore, that the world would be a better place if we all followed it. Yet many—if not most—do not routinely follow it. We may claim to—and we certainly want others to—but we do not actually follow it. We are cognizant of the golden rule, we sense the imperative to follow it, yet few live according to it. Why is this?

The short answer is that following the golden rule is hard and will lead to hardship. We doubt whether life will go well for us if we follow the golden rule; we think that life will be more difficult and more costly for those who follow the golden rule than for those who don't. So while I know that I should follow the golden rule, I also know that many won't, and that this will disadvantage me. It would be good for me if *others* did (and if *they thought I* did), and so I will tout its virtues, encouraging them to do so—crossing my fingers that there is a critical mass of those who do. Deep down, though, I think that routinely following the golden rule will be harmful, even destructive to me. While many might start on the moral path as far as "*not* doing to others . . .," the next step of "*doing* as we would be done by" is a step too far because it exposes us to hardship and risks. Our attitude seems to be, "You go first." Consequently, few find the courage to take the leap. We are glad to be "free riders" and wait for others to take the first step.

It is certainly true that following the golden rule will be hard given the way the world is. It is tempting to think, then, that following the golden rule must be at odds with the way the world really is, or that it is not realistic, and that other rules actually govern the real world, such as "Pursue happiness," and "The fittest survive." We might conclude, as we noted in the last section, that the problem must be with the rule itself. "Maybe it is not a rule but only a guideline, not an imperative but an option. Maybe, given the difficulty in following the golden rule, it is really the law of self-preservation that holds true."

Is it true that the golden rule does not accord with the real world? One objective of this essay is to propose a worldview where the answers to the questions, "What can we know?," "What should we do?," and "What might we hope for?" align. If our answer to how we should live conflicts with how the world really is, our lives will be disjointed, we will be unable to marshal our full capabilities and focus on common goals, and it will be as though we live in different worlds.

The answer to the question "How should we live?," we have argued, is that we ought to follow the golden rule. Why? *Just because* this rule aligns with what's really going on in the world. Given the widespread corruption and destructiveness in our world and their tendency to spread and escalate, we cannot stay stuck in the rut of self-preservation or fall into the pursuit of happiness, both of which lead to conflict. The golden rule, therefore, is not a standard applying only to a few or an ideal rising too high for most, but an imperative for all of us. The danger that conflict can escalate out of control and result in the ruin of societies is too great to do anything less. To stand idly by or turn a blind eye to the corruption and violence before us is to risk that they increase and spread with destructive potential beyond anything humans have ever experienced.

In the next part, we will argue that following the path that starts with the silver rule leads to the love of others, where self-serving interests are displaced, where we no longer ask "What's in it for me?," and where we find that love is a path to be pursued for its own sake. The truth about the apparent conflict between self-serving interests and other-regard is that love really is the law of life: it is "love that makes the world go round." If we have faith that love is the law of life, life and love might prevail in the end; but if we give in to lives of self-interest, neither love nor life will survive.

Religious believers of many types will claim that we ought to follow the golden rule, but for different reasons. Many Christians, for example, will say that they follow the golden rule because God commanded it. They do so out of obedience to God, or as a demonstration of their trust in God's promise of a closer relationship in this life and in the life to come. With such belief, they live according to the golden rule less because it aligns with relationships in this earthly life but more with their spiritual life.

In that case, though, we have to ask whether we would be following the golden rule as a means to another end—if, that is to say, we were actually looking past this world and the people in it. Wouldn't we be using the lives of others primarily as a means for obtaining our own spiritual or otherworldly ends? If we are more concerned for our own souls than with others' lives, our moral actions would not be genuine, and others would sense our duplicity. They would sense that we are following the golden rule not for them but for ourselves; not because it is to be followed for its own sake but because it is a means to our own spiritual or otherworldly ends. The reason we should follow the golden rule, rather, is because it is what there is for us to do in *this* life, given the way our world is.

This becomes even clearer when we see the way many Christians understand their failure to follow the golden rule and the consequences of not following it. If they have fallen short of the golden rule and wronged others, they turn to God—not others—for forgiveness, and they receive it simply by asking for it. That is the way many understand forgiveness today. All they need to do is ask God's forgiveness—which is certain—and they need to do nothing more to atone for what they did or did not do. Little thought is given to asking for forgiveness from others or reconciling with them. It is really the vertical relationship with God that matters, not the horizontal relationship with the persons wronged. If that did matter, forgiveness would involve more than simply asking God for it but actually turning one's life around, as well as making amends and repairing others' lives. It may be difficult or impossible always to right the wrong, make amends, or stop the destructive ramifications of what I have done or failed to do, but that is what this-worldly forgiveness entails. We seem to think, rather, that God will overlook the ill we have done to others or to nature, therefore we need not make amends or atone for our actions. As long as my relationship with God is good, accounting for the consequences of my actions on others isn't a concern. Besides, since the consequences of my actions in the world have no ultimate significance for me or the world that is passing away, it doesn't really matter that I make amends or "settle up."

Given the way many Christians understand forgiveness today, we can see that, for them, it is enough that I *try* to follow the golden rule. *Actually* following it does not matter. What counts for God is that I *try*. So I convince myself that I am making a good effort. My relationship to God is more important than my relationship to Earthlings; consequently, I cultivate the former more than I work on the latter. God will forgive all my moral shortcomings, and my relationship with God will remain intact. Since many actively anticipate their existence apart from Earth anyway, their identity is not rooted in it, not really borne of the Earth. It follows that we are also above earthly morality and mortality, not defined by it. This is another reason why it is tempting to view their time on Earth as only a temporary sojourn.

At the end of the day, to conclude, whether I am a materialist or a theist, it does not really matter whether I lead a morally principled life or not. Materialists see no hope for the world whatever we do since it is destined for destruction. As far as my own life is concerned, I can have a happy life if I play my cards right: gain sufficient material resources, pursue my opportunities, make shrewd use of my relationships, avoid others' troubles, etc. (This will prove difficult, though, for beings with our moral senses. We will have to suppress them to live that way, and we will have to ignore the destructive consequences of lives lived for the pursuit of material gain.) For the theist, too, this world will not last, and all the bad consequences and ill-effects my behavior has on the world won't matter in the end. My good relationship with God is certain, however god-awful my worldly relationships, and my relationship to God is what really matters in the long run anyway. (This way of thinking, though, will not satisfy self-critical souls who think that "God knows what is in my heart." There will be no end to disturbing questions, such as, "Am I *really* good with God? Am I *truly* sincere when I repent and ask for forgiveness? Am I kidding myself?")

Why should I live according to moral rules? Not to be nice, not to impress others, not to make points with God, but because, given what's going on in the world, it is what there is for us to do. We should orient our lives by moral rules because they accord with what is true about our world: that darkness is real and active, and that life is threatened with unceasing disordering. It is wishful thinking—not hope—to try to avoid it or escape it. We should not suppose that we can implore God to suspend the laws of nature, stop the course of events, and spare us from it. It is by following moral rules that we to face up to this, and this gives us hope for our world.

But now, since the destructive forces arrayed against us are so formidable, what real hope is there? Why follow the golden rule, enduring the sacrifices that would result, if following it cannot prevail against those forces? We need a special kind of hope to take that leap. If we can have faith that there is a source that initiated the creation of the universe, and that it is purposeful, intending to bring light and life out of dark lifelessness, then we might have hope that it will prevail. The ascendance of moral living over barbarism, too, especially the power of love to prevail over corruption and violence, can give us hope that the source giving rise to moral living was love and that it is active in the world, inspiring us to do the same. We can have hope, then, if we believe that love has been at work from the beginning, opposing chaos, freeing the world from captivity to pointless disorder so that living things and intelligent beings can exist, and because, ultimately, love works.

PART THREE

PART THREE

III

What Might We Hope?

WE ARE FREE

In posing the question "What should we do?," we assume we have minds free to propose answers—good and bad—and wills free to act upon them—successfully or not. Even though we may be pressured by many factors pressing upon us to behave in predictable ways, we are not compelled to behave in any particular way. We are beings who can generate their own thoughts and who are responsible for their own actions; we are not simply animals or creatures driven to behave in predetermined or predestined ways. Neither the claim that a person is an animal whose behavior is determined by natural laws nor the belief that a person is a creature created out of nothing whose life is predestined by an omnipotent, omniscient Creator can account for minds and wills that are free. This is a complex issue, of course. In the worldview we are envisioning, though, we assert that we are free.[1]

To assert that we are free conforms with the common practice of holding one another responsible for our actions and affirms our sense of moral responsibility. It is an understandable assumption, though it is one

---

1. For example, Daniel Dennett gives a materialist's denial of free will in *Consciousness Explained* ("You are made of robots"; 33). Luther gives a theist's denial of free will in Rupp, *Luther and Erasmus* ("God is omnipotent, not only in power, but also in action. . . . Otherwise he would be a ridiculous God. . . . He knows and foreknows all things . . . so we do not do anything by right of free choice"; 244–45).

neither the materialist nor the theist can grant. In the first place, we hold one another responsible for our actions because we assume we are free: our emotions *discover* human needs, our minds *create* moral responses, and our wills *shape* the world—all in *novel, self-critical* ways. That way of thinking best accounts for our sense of responsibility and the many experiences associated with it: petition from one person and obligation for the other; outrage in one case and shame on the other; praise from one and humility for the other; guilt and forgiveness; atonement and reconciliation; etc. We cannot account for such experiences if we think individuals simply behave according to the same probabilities that govern all matter; and we cannot make that claim if we think individuals are simply creatures created out of nothing who behave the way their omnipotent, omniscient Creator predestined them to. The worldview we are developing can because it follows from this view of the creation of the cosmos: the creation was a free act to deliver—to free—the world from chaos for the purpose of generating living things and intelligent beings who could, in a similar way, protect the creation from chaos and preserve it.

Materialism, furthermore, cannot explain how brains, behaving according to material laws, become minds directing thoughts and conduct, even manipulating their own brains. It cannot explain how glucose achieves self-consciousness. Theism, in a similar way, cannot explain how creatures could ever be free of the control of their Creator. It is incomprehensible how a supreme being—omnipotent and omniscient—could make creatures from nothing—creating the very material out of which they are made, putting everything they are into them—and not determine how they would behave, or make them "free." If materialism and theism do not provide adequate explanations for our capacity to be free, how should we understand it?

We cannot claim to be free if we are no more than containers of chemicals or pots made by a pot maker. A worldview makes room for freedom when it denies that our world is either merely matter in random motion, or simply created from nothing by an omniscient and omnipotent Creator. To fill in that space, we might say that matter alone is simply potential, formless and inert, or in a confused state, incapable of realizing its potential without being informed. The universe as we know it began when matter was formed by principles that allowed it to evolve and realize its potential, or when it was delivered from formlessness. Those principles informing matter ordered it according to regularities and constancies, and freed matter from the chaos of useless misinformation so it could actualize its potential over billions of years and in uncountable ways. In humans, those principles generated beings who could reason, who had self-awareness, and who could act freely. The evolution of human beings from matter, then, was neither random nor predestined but freely initiated and mindfully guided. This better accounts for the reality of an ordered and purposive universe, as well as the reality of human freedom. That, in broad strokes, is how we would account for our capacity to be free.

The creation was a free act to deliver formless matter from chaos so that it could become a cosmos with living things that could evolve into intelligent beings who could themselves protect life and promote its development. Our capacity to act freely stems from the free act to initiate the creation. That's the source of our freedom, and human beings truly realize their freedom when they do the same. Considering that an initial act freed bound potential by instilling it with ordering principles, we can understand how that potential could blossom into human freedom. Our wonder before the world and our drive to understand it, as well as our respect for human life and our responsibility for it, are all manifestations of this emancipating act. Our purpose, furthermore, is to utilize that capacity for freedom. It might lie dormant, it might be neglected, it might be abused, it might be hijacked by instincts, it might be restricted by others, but it can be drawn upon, prompted, stimulated, and activated when we have the proper worldview or a compelling way to understand our place in the world.

We best account for human life when we believe that we have minds able to know what is really going on in the world, hearts able to grasp what needs to be done to promote life and oppose corruption and destruction, and wills with the power to act. We can know what is real and act on it: we can be objective—see past subjective factors—and act freely—not be compelled by natural and social conditions. We are free when we utilize those uniquely human capacities—mind, emotions, willpower—that allow us to oppose corruption and violence, as well as preserve, protect, and promote life.

As we discussed in the last section, we have the potential—the mind, the emotions, the willpower—to live according to moral principles. When we do that, when we look outside of ourselves to what is actually happening in the lives of others, we cannot help but see how many are not free, and how many have not been able to develop those capacities. It might be that they are denied the opportunity, it might be that they have squandered their opportunities—as we ourselves have failed to develop our own minds, emotions, and wills. It might be that they are oppressed and do not have the opportunity. Whatever the case may be, when we make that principled move, we cannot help but see their plight and be drawn to help. We actualize our own potential when we do for others as they would have us do for them—which is to help them develop their minds, emotions, and wills—so that they, too, can live according to moral principles. We realize our freedom not when we do whatever we want but when we help free others from the constraints that limit their freedom. We know freedom is real because we help others be free.

We argued in the last section that we live out our humanity and realize our freedom by following moral rules. It is just because the world is in the threatened state that it is that following them is what there is for us to do. They should be followed for their own sake, therefore, not because to do so serves my interests in this world (as in materialism), or for life in another (as in theism). The moral initiative, then, is less a "call to duty" than the realization of what "needs to be done." It is not so much a "demand to obey" than an invitation to open my eyes to respond to what's in front of me; less something I am "supposed to do" than something to be done for its own sake.

Realizing our freedom by following moral rules fulfills our purpose in life. We see this in sharp relief when we consider the opposite: enslavement, human beings denying other human beings their freedom. No action realizes our purpose in life more than helping others be free; the greatest denial of our humanity, conversely, is depriving others of theirs. When we see that, we recognize how essential freedom is for our identity and how deeply our dignity is rooted in it. Whatever doubt we might have concerning our capacity to be free, imagine how enraged we would be if we were enslaved; imagine the outrage we would feel toward those who enslaved us.

Subjugating human beings, denying them the opportunity to exercise and develop their capabilities—dismissing their dignity, in other words—is a deplorable abuse of one's freedom over another. That is why few things arouse moral outrage as much as slavery. Slavery reveals the chasm between the use of freedom to preserve, protect, and promote life—what we should see as the high point in the history of the universe—and its abuse to enslave life—the low point. It is wonderful to see people develop and use their freedom to help others be free. Conversely, it is dreadful to see people abuse their freedom to suppress and destroy the minds, hearts, and wills of others—even their own—worsening our enslavements and increasing the violence in our world. It is dreadful to witness the suppression of beings who are capable of living free, principled lives. That is why slavery is so abhorrent. As Kant put it, "Nothing can be more appalling than that the action of a human stand under the will of another. Hence no abhorrence can be more natural than that which a person has against servitude."[2]

We even consider slavery a "crime against *humanity*," not only against the enslaved. It is a crime because it holds human potential in bondage, preventing it from realizing its natural purposes. Slavery is a great wrong and must be challenged because it holds human beings' unique capacities—the

---

2. Guyer, *Kant*, 10–11.

bases of their dignity—captive to purposeless existence. Because that is so, it is a wrong committed not only against the enslaved but against all of us.

Slavery not only wrongs the enslaved, then, but all human beings. It also corrupts the enslavers, and it shames all who witness it and do nothing to help those subjugated by it. Slavery is a scourge on all of us, one that we are obligated to oppose. We are moved to free the enslaved from that indignity not only for their sake but for our own self-respect and for all humanity. Any deliverance from it at all, however costly to obtain, is better than abject subjugation to it. We understand, then, when we read in slave narratives, "Death is better than slavery." Better to die trying to escape slavery than not to try and to remain in servitude. Deliverance from slavery, importantly, is a central theme in the biblical view we are developing, and we will return to it in the last section.[3]

The perplexity here is that we have the capacities to preserve life, protect human beings, and promote human dignity—to help others realize their potential to be free—yet too often we remain stuck in self-serving interests—in servitude, as we discussed above, to various pursuits of happiness, merely following our animal impulses, or lulled into a belief in our immortality. We have the capacity to be free, yet too often we do not use that capacity, with the result that we become unfree, captive to instincts and impulses that create more destruction than living things do that do not have that capacity.

There is irony and tragedy in this. We give away our free will and become slaves to desires and dreams. We could say that we subvert freedom by enslaving ourselves. We are free, but choose bondage instead. We are tempted by the pursuit of happiness and self-preservation to become what we are not—animals and angels, not moral mortals. We use our freedom to abdicate our freedom. Rather than use it to preserve, protect, and promote life, we act to foster and abet threats to life. We even use our freedom to take away the freedom of others.

We *can* be free. We can be free from the blind drive for self-preservation and the mindless pursuit of happiness. We *are* free when we exercise those capacities—our minds, hearts, and wills—in principled living, when we do for others as they would have us do for them. Our problem, our "original sin," is that we vacate those capacities and so abdicate our freedom. In various ways we do *not use* it, or we *misuse* it, or we *abuse* it. Tempted to live the amoral life of animals, we do *not use* our freedom. Tempted to use our moral capacities to reach immortal ends, we *misuse* use our moral capabilities, endeavoring to leave this world for another. Tempted to live

3. Douglass, *Narrative*, 84; Jacobs, *Incidents*, 189.

like immortal gods, we also *abuse* our creative abilities, exercising destructive powers, "lording it over" others. In all these ways we are tempted to be something we are not. The result is that we foster the conflicts that accompany the blind drive for self-preservation and foment the corruption that follows the mindless pursuit of happiness.

As we discussed above, we do *not use* our freedom when we behave like animals, simply preserving ourselves and pursuing happiness; and we *misuse* freedom when we set our eyes on otherworldly ends. But also, the more we disengage from the moral life—innocently wanting not to "cause any trouble," to "do no harm," to "keep to ourselves" and simply to "satisfy our own needs"—the more corruption and animosities creep into our common life. When we *do not use* our moral capabilities, they weaken, and we succumb to the mere pursuit of happiness with the jealousies, competition, and animosities that result. We also become bound to strategies of self-preservation and so more firmly entrenched on paths leading to violence and destruction. When we do not exercise our capacities to live the life of moral, mortal human beings, in other words, we allow our capacity for freedom to atrophy. The less we exercise our moral capabilities, the weaker they become, the less able we are to oppose corruption and violence, and the more destructiveness dominates our lives. When we abdicate our freedom to fulfill moral responsibilities, the harder it is to restore it and get it back.

Finally, we *abuse* our freedom when we become destructive. Human beings have it within themselves to do needlessly destructive things. Subverting what it means to be like god, we become anti-gods in that we use those capabilities to destroy rather than create. If I am honest with myself, there are times when I choose to be destructive just to be destructive—even though there is no benefit to me. There are times when I would rather hurt than help, rather undermine another's self-worth and undercut their dignity than upbuild it. We all can imagine such occasions. We can even imagine circumstances where we could act violently with no moral justification. While we may be averse to destructiveness and not have the stomach for violence, there are times when we desire its effects. In that way we support violence, or we vote for those who promote it, even though we may not be violent ourselves. In these ways I do not promote constructive work in the world but destructiveness instead.

How do we account for this? It is not adequate to explain this human propensity by singling out peculiar psychological traits, or particular social circumstances, or individual pathologies. What we require is a general explanation that accounts for more than what *he* did, or for what *those people* do, but that accounts for what *all* of us—me included—are capable of doing.

We need an explanation that shows how we all have it within ourselves to do needlessly destructive things.

That general explanation, discussed in the previous part, is that we know we should live the lives of the moral mortals we are, actively following moral principles, but that we do not persistently do so. Instead, we live like amoral animals and immortal gods with the result that the corruption and violence in our world persists and chaos advances. That is how we might understand what original sin is. In biblical terms, we are created in the Creator's likeness to be good stewards of the creation, advancing the Creator's purpose. Too often, though, we allow ourselves to become instruments of the chaos that is undermining the creation.

In addition to the abuse of freedom and the chaos of active destruction, to conclude, there is also the more subtle chaos of dissolution, where inactivity and inertness contribute to the general decline of human life. The universe appears headed toward a chaos of inactivity, of useless energy, where nothing can come from it. And it seems that humans, too, slide into a state of useless inactivity—or at least, they want to. Just as entropy is pulling the universe toward a state where energy becomes useless, so too our desires often aim for that state as well.

Insofar as I prefer rest over work and avocation over vocation, aiming to live in a state of ease, I am moving toward the same state of inactivity. In that way the goal of my life mirrors the end of the universe brought about by entropy. If that is what I am striving for, if that is really where I want to be, then the end for me is the same as for the formless void. We are moving in the same direction and toward the same state. In this case it's not so much that I want to destroy and eliminate something but that I want the absence of something, of anything that puts a demand on me. I want the nothing of inaction, of not being expected to do anything. In effect, I am allying myself with the chaos of spent energy, of energy no longer capable of doing anything. I am falling in line with the futility of aimlessness and so of impotence, of the incapacity for constructive development of any kind.

This is the chaos not of a destructive state but of an inert one, where, I imagine, I can just be, exist, not have to do anything but enjoy myself, whether that be satisfying my natural desires or comforting myself with supernatural wishes. It's biding my time, not using it for good, not troubling myself to contend with others' privations and urgencies. It's withdrawing from our common life, taking in without giving out, working less and less and resting more and more. It's retiring early so more time and more energy is spent on vacation, recreation, and traveling: not time to recreate for renewed activity or rest to restore for continued work but a permanent state of rest, of doing nothing but existing, taking in the resources needed to exist but giving nothing in return. This happens when I promote the useless frittering away of time and energy, squandering resources rather than using them constructively, when I want to receive more than I contribute. In this way I advance the world's steady decline into a state of dissolution.

We can be drawn into the disorder of purposelessness that results from avoiding purpose, from not using our freedom constructively. After all, if the universe has no purpose, why should I have one? Isn't the universe itself heading toward just that kind of useless energy? We can be duped into thinking that the goal of life is rest and relaxation—the sooner the better, now and forever. Living in a state of doing nothing to sustain life in our world leads us to the very same end: a state where I use up more than I produce or take in and return nothing—a net loss in the energy transfer of life. I take the path of ease, and not just for a temporary recreation or rest but for perpetual life on the beach, or perpetual dithering where I accomplish little, or for early retirement where I do nothing. We can be tempted to live like that, aiding the cause of chaos. In that way, too, we abdicate our freedom and advance chaos's own end: uselessness.

Many believers, similarly, think that the universe exists only as a first stage for souls as they prepare themselves for eternal rest in their heavenly home. If our souls eventually will have eternal rest with God, why not enjoy a foretaste of that endless peace now? God rested on the Sabbath day, the high point of creation; why shouldn't we have the same goal and do the same? Believing this way, we can begin to think that we work in order to rest, the goal being to work fewer and fewer days and rest more and more days, weeks, months, years. We seek the nothing of inaction, of not having to get anywhere, do anything, of not having to make anything of ourselves.

In Part One we saw that it is best to see the creation of the universe as the deliverance of energy from captivity to chaos, from the disordering that keeps the universe from realizing its potential and now threatens it with final disintegration. We can also see that human existence as well needs to be freed from those destructive tendencies that, if not opposed, will lead to a similar end. What keeps human existence from that fate is living principled lives—creative acts in their own right—because they help free human life from captivity to the disorders we described. Because of the threats posed by corruption and violence, it takes courage to live moral lives. It requires, we might say, a leap. To make that move, and to help others develop their capacities and be free from hostilities and oppression, require a leap of courage and hope.

As discussed at the end of Part Two, it will take courage because it will cost us. Because that is so, we shrink from doing what we know we should do. Understandably so. It is difficult for me to tune out my anxious cries to secure my own safety or insistent pleas to satisfy my own desires. But if we can, and when we do—when we heed the call to look out for others—we will find that we hear those nagging self-centered pleas less and less, and a quiet self-forgetting takes its place more and more.

Sometimes we are able to live according to moral principles by helping others in need—the chief need being to realize their potential to be free—defying the threats posed to our wellbeing and risking the costs we might incur. How do we come to do that? It requires courage to overcome self-serving interests. That only happens when we act without asking, "What's in it for me?," but spontaneously. It happens when we do not credit our acts in some register of good deeds, adding to our own merit, but become oblivious to them. It happens, in other words, when it becomes the natural thing to do. And that happens when we have a compelling worldview demonstrating what is really going on in the world and what there is for us to do in it. The worldview we are developing aims to do that. From its perspective we are able to get outside ourselves, broaden our perspective on life, and see what needs doing. When we do that, we contribute to an ongoing creation, and we thwart those factors working to destroy it. Just as the creation was an act to deliver potential from futile existence, so too following moral principles works to deliver human potential from futile lives.

Can we honestly have hope for this world, though, if looming over us is the violent end to the Earth and eventually the universe? Matter itself may be no more, and all potential to realize anything may be lost forever. If the universe has no future, what can we realistically hope for? We will address this question in the next section.

WHAT MIGHT WE HOPE FOR THIS WORLD?

What can we know? What ought we do? What might we hope for? As discussed earlier, when answers to these questions align, we have a coherent worldview, and we can focus our lives on realistic, worthy goals. Our worldview is constructive when our convictions concerning what is really going on in the world orient our lives and ground our hopes. When they do not align, it will seem as though we exist in disconnected dimensions without a worldview at all; then our lives will be disjointed and we will be unable to move toward consistent ends. We will limp through life unable to move resolutely toward realistic goals. We have discussed answers to the first two questions, taking the position that, given the lawfulness of the natural world, we can be confident in our knowledge of the world; and, given the moral rules emerging from our history, we can have confidence in how we should live. Now, what might we hope for this world?

Given what we know and what we don't know to be true about life and the way we should live, what might we hope for in this life? What is an intellectually honest, responsible hope for our future? We should reiterate that neither materialism nor theism have hope for *this* world: there can be no hope for this world if it is merely matter, or if heaven or some spiritual reality is set to replace this world. If matter is all there is, then it looks as though it may simply exhaust itself and come to nothing. Or, if the creation has been predestined for destruction by the Creator, then again, there is no hope for this world. With these forbidding accounts of the destiny of the universe, what can we hope for?

Our answer to "What may we hope for?" needs to connect to what we know and what we should do, coordinating our understanding and actions; otherwise, we are not speaking of hope but of wishes or dreams. If, that is to say, we answer, "You can hope for anything you want," we have to ask whether we are dealing with hope at all or only with fantasies disconnected from what we know to be true and with how we should live. If we thought that natural laws were "made up" and that scientific knowledge did not help us gain a firmer and firmer grip on reality, or that moral rules were "merely subjective and relative" and that there were no moral truths, then yes, we might "hope" for any future we want, one where all our dreams can come true. Intellectually honest, responsible hope, though, gives real direction to our lives because it is framed by our natural knowledge and our moral insights.

The answer to "What may we hope for?," then, cannot be "anything we want" because then hopes would be no different from wishes or dreams. Hoping is not wishing because to hope is actively to take steps toward an attainable, not merely thinkable, future. Otherwise our lives today have no connection with the world tomorrow. In the real world, not all dreams can come true. What can we hope for when we are serious about the future of *this* world, not merely some *thinkable* world, when we are concerned about *our* world, not *private* dream worlds?

It is easy, though, to get the idea today that we are permitted to believe in any future we want, in whatever helps us cope with this world, not in what helps us sustain or improve it. Hopes today can be irrational wishes, disconnected from what we actually know and how we should live our lives to improve the world. Today you can hope that after death you will go to a heavenly paradise, or forever relive the happiest moments in your life, or spend eternity with the lover of your choice, or exist in one of an infinite number of parallel universes, or go back in time to reign over your royal court. No one is allowed to challenge these "hopes" because you are permitted to hope for anything you want, in whatever helps you cope—whether or not your hope connects with how we should live or what we know to be true about life. We seem to think that all our dreams can come true, that wishing for something can make it so, and that the distant future can conform to our desires. Finally, then, it doesn't matter what happens to this world or what you do in this life because the next life can be whatever you want it to be.

If our ultimate concerns are those we discussed in the last part—pursuing happiness and preserving ourselves—this makes perfect sense because then we will try not simply to find happiness in this life or preserve ourselves in this life but in future lives as well. Tempted to think we are like gods who will not die, we believe something more awaits us. It could be heaven. It could be existence in some spiritual dimension of this universe. It could be life in some other universe. We think we can have any of these just for the believing or just for the wishing.

Coupled with such dreams and wishes, if we also maintained that this world was doomed, that there was no hope for our world, then we would have no incentive to work to improve it, and our desire would simply be to make the most of life while we could. "Hope" for this world would be reduced to optimism: attaining objectives within the span of my own life—which probably comes back to making myself as secure, comfortable, and happy as I can. "Hope," then, would have no more significant goal than our pursuit of happiness or our drive to preserve ourselves. If we maintained that the world had no future, that it would be destroyed and come to nothing—that nature had an expiration date, as it were—and that all our achievements and insights would amount to nothing in the end, then our attitude and efforts to improve our world surely would be deflated and undercut. Or, if we believed that our hope is in a spiritual world, we might think that our efforts now aim to secure an otherworldly goal after this life—but we would have no hope for this world. If, as we mentioned above, I think that rituals, worship, prayer, and obedience are the activities that will secure my place in heaven, then it is likely that I will be less concerned with moral problems in this world than with immortality in the next. Either way, there will be little connection between our efforts now and the future of this world.

Hope for this world for materialists, then, comes down to chance, a matter of luck. To hope is to cross your fingers that events break your way, that you are fortunate enough to have the material resources, opportunities, and advantages that enable you to avoid hardships and that put you ahead in the pursuit of happiness. Hope for this world for theists is that God will spare them many of this world's sufferings and eventually take them out of it to a better one. In either case, such hope would do nothing to stop the spread of corruption and violence in this world, and may even aid it.

We should start the discussion by reiterating that hope in the future is built on confidence in our knowledge of the present and past. We have confidence in our present knowledge, that is to say, because we have convictions about the way the world is that have proven to be fruitful. This confidence rests on beliefs about our world that we think are well founded, have stood the test of time, and so are worth keeping.

Why are the sciences so successful? Why can we place our confidence in them? These questions deserve answers. There must be a reason the sciences work as well as they do, and it is better to come to terms with why the sciences are so successful than to stop asking these basic questions or to silence a legitimate curiosity. While we may not be able to answer those questions with certainty, we can generate reasonable beliefs that are adequate to our natural interest in these questions. Such reasonable beliefs can broaden our understanding, connecting our insights into other vital aspects of our lives, such as the arts, ethics, and religion. Such beliefs, moreover, can inspire us to probe the reason for our existence and its purpose, surely a legitimate concern.

Our confidence, as we discussed in Part One, stems from convictions or working assumptions pertaining to the uniformity, constancies, and harmonies of nature. Several of these assumptions are that matter behaves the same on Earth as it does light-years away, that the regularities we observe now continue throughout time, and that the natural world is a whole of interrelated parts. Without these assumptions, scientific investigation would flounder and would not yield the comprehensive understanding it does. These convictions concerning what we know, furthermore, connect with our other questions—what should we do, and what we might hope for? It enriches human life, for reasons we have already discussed, when our beliefs concerning what we know to be true of the world connect with how we should live and what we might hope for. Our worldview is constructive when our convictions concerning what we can know orient our lives and ground our hopes.

Parallel to our confidence in the natural sciences is our confidence in the social sciences. We believe that our past resembles our present so that we can gain an understanding of our history; and we believe that we can construct rules governing human behavior so that we can discern the helpful from the unhelpful, the functional from the dysfunctional. Put another way, we do not think that understanding our past and present is only a matter of opinion—merely subjective or relative. More specifically, the historical record shows us how living a principled life fulfills the purpose of human life, as well as how ignoring or opposing it diminishes it. To the concerns at issue, this means that we can have confidence in moral judgments—that they are not merely opinions. Our experience warrants the belief that we know how to do better and have properly extended our ethical concerns further and further and to more and more—even though we often fail to do what we know we should. Principled ethical actions improve debased behavior, stop ruthlessness, and keep us from descending back into the brutish existence our history records.

It is because there are these natural uniformities, constancies, and harmonies that matter organizes and forms into increasingly complex structures that provide stability over time and space, allowing humans to purposively organize their lives. It makes sense to think that there is a reason for this, that an originating initiative gave rise to this development. Biblical theology has maintained that the principled informing that forms the world is the wisdom of a Creator active from the beginning and throughout time and space. Evolution, from that perspective, is the result of this initiative that continues to be active throughout the material world and in us. From our point of view, these convictions concerning the orderliness of the natural world invite the idea that there is something more going on in it than the random coming together and coming apart of matter. There is some larger content—something superordinate—to be "read off" of these regularities and trajectories that informs what is going on in the world. The biblical view we are proposing is that these regularities suggest something mindful and the purposiveness something willful. Something understandable, in short, is taking place within the world as a whole.

We have confidence, then, in our knowledge of the natural world; but we also know what we do not know. We have confidence, that is, in our understanding of how matter on the cosmological scale behaves; but we also understand that that knowledge pertains to only 5 percent of the universe, other forms of matter and energy being unknown to us. This gives us reason to hesitate about prognostications concerning the end of the universe. When dark matter and dark energy are better understood, we might discover that the universe will not come to nothing; it might be that purposive ordering, such as we find in the known universe, is also at work there. That would brighten our prospects and reorient what we might look forward to.

Since 95 percent of the matter in the universe is unknown to us, it may be that our long-term future will not be as bleak as it seems, and that the life-giving order we see on Earth will extend into the future. Perhaps we will be able to transform nature to further support life; perhaps human life can exist beyond the Earth; perhaps we will overcome the corrosive effects of entropy; perhaps other intelligent life in the universe has found ways to secure the future. These are things we do not know but might reasonably consider. More importantly, we know that we have the ability to live principled lives and that we have been able to thwart corruption and violence; we can, in short, choose life over death, costly though that may be. This gives us hope that we will choose to sustain life rather than destroy it.[4]

To review, then, the history and destiny of the universe as best we know it. The universe began in a virtual nothingness—a "formless void," as the Bible imagined it—and it may well end in nothingness. In between, life evolved out of this lifelessness, developing—only on Earth, as far as we know—into beings capable of knowing this history and capable of using their own lives to protect, preserve, and promote other living things. In broad outline, then, there is evident purposiveness in this trajectory, but it is contested, so much so that nothingness or a "formless void" may be the end result. It is not adequate to say that this is just the way matter behaves—giving birth to life and then killing itself. And it does not make sense to say that a supreme being would create the universe, pronounce it very good, love it, become incarnate in it—and then destroy it. Human beings, furthermore, who can protect life and promote their own lives, are just as capable of wantonly destroying other life, as well as their own. How do we make sense of this? How do we account for what's going on? Is there a reasonable account to give of this overview?

The proposal is that when we look at the origin and destiny of the universe in this light, the superintending concept that comes into view is *deliverance*. It is a constructive, fruitful idea to see the beginning of the cosmos as a deliberate act that delivered the universe from chaos, freeing matter from captivity to a futile existence. To put it abstractly: something is freed from something by something for something. Creation was a mindful, willful, and empathetic act to release formless matter frozen in purposeless existence so that it could actualize its potential, and evolution is the continuation of that action. On this account the creation is the freeing of matter *from* chaos *for* realizing its potential to become a cosmos with living things and intelligent beings. It is the purposeful drive to oppose chaos and establish a cosmos that upholds life over lifelessness and that gives rise to beings who themselves protect the orders that sustain life, preserve life from lifelessness, and promote life that can continue the creation.

Typically, we imagine that the creation was an effortless, solitary act. "The creation" conjures up visions of a heavenly king pronouncing a royal edict, effortlessly designing and establishing the universe. This is the idea of God as a heavenly architect we see in the Bible. In a similar way, when

---

4. Michio Kaku explores such possibilities in *Future of Humanity*.

we think of God as a heavenly king, emancipating slaves from slavery or delivering a whole people from bondage, we imagine redemption as a single act that costs the king nothing. In the view we are developing, by contrast, creation is not effortless because it is done in the face of opposition. Redemption as well—freeing humanity from corruption and violence—was not effortless but costly, from the point of view of the Christian Scriptures.

An overview of the Bible shows that the theme of deliverance had a guiding role to play. Deliverance from Egypt, to take an important episode, was a defining moment in the history of Israel. The Lord freed the Israelites *from* servitude to Pharaoh, the god of Egypt, *for* service to the Lord, the God of their ancestors. Passing through the deep, chaotic waters of the Red Sea—a theme repeated in the account of the creation out of the deep darkness—they are delivered from slavery and given laws to live by in order to live as God's people. Their history is the story of their successes and failures in living up to that law, underscored by prophets who warn them of the consequences of failure to live by those moral principles. The Christian Scriptures continue this story when Jesus comes not "to abolish [the law and the prophets] but to fulfill" (Matt 5:17) and to oppose the religious tyranny and political servitude that subjugated the people of Israel in order that they might live as God intended. This theme—freedom *from* captivity *for* freedom to live the way God intended people to live—is one way to chart the way the Bible understands the nature of God and the destiny of his people. It also, we can see, sheds light on our understanding of the creation and evolution of the universe. The creation itself is the freeing of matter from a state of chaos so that it could generate its potential and become an ordered cosmos. From this vantage point, deliverance pertains not only to humanity but to the whole creation.

Israel's history centered on deliverance: the way out of bondage toward freedom. We can see the history of creation in a parallel way: from lifelessness toward life. And we can see our own lives from the same point of view: a moral journey continually turning away from the pull of self-centeredness toward principled living that protects, preserves, and promotes life. It takes work, we know, to overcome the gravity of self-centeredness pulling us inward and to move outward toward the needs of the world outside us.

The writers of Exodus and Genesis wrote as though God's deliverance was effortless. Miracle after miracle showed that Pharaoh and even the Red Sea were no match for the Lord. So too, in the beginning, God merely spoke and the deep darkness was dispersed. It's a different story for Christian writers. The Messiah comes to deliver his people from religious oppression, political tyranny, and the powers of sin and death, but those very powers conspire to kill him. To illustrate this difference further, in Genesis God breathes over the waters, initiating the creation, and later breathes into Adam, giving him life. In John's Gospel, similarly, Jesus gives over his breath to his followers—but it is in dying that he imparts his life. In the former instances imparting the life-giving spirit seems effortless; in the latter, it is by giving up his life that Jesus's Spirit passes into others. "Very truly, I tell you, unless a grain of wheat falls into the earth and dies, it remains just a single grain; but if it dies, it bears much fruit" (John 12:24). The new life comes at a cost.

Jesus's followers believed that his life and death revealed what was really going on in the world: there was a struggle between the kingdom of God and hostile forces; Jesus came to oppose corruption and violence with love; love would prevail. Violent powers were corrupting, enslaving, and destroying life, and they must be subdued, opposed, and defeated. It required action to "set my people free," or to "subdue the strong man," or to defeat "sin, death, and the power of the devil," and came with a cost. These death-dealing powers had to be overcome in order for humanity to be free to live-out its purpose. In Jesus's case it was to free people *from* religious corruption, moral complacency, political oppression, economic deprivation, and military tyranny *for* living into the kingdom of God.

Jesus's followers believed, furthermore, that Jesus's life and death gave the best insight into God's nature. Jesus's crucifixion, especially, prompted intense theological reflection. "Why was it necessary that the Messiah suffer and be killed?" That the Son of God was crucified showed that God was not unaffected by the conflict with the powers of evil. Delivering humanity from corruption and violence cost God. Because opposition to God is real, the love of God that delivers us from it is costly. In some way, theologians reasoned, God died to save humanity.

If Jesus's life and death is the clearest insight into God, the expenditure of life to redeem life repeats the expenditure of life to create life. The cost to deliver life from corruption and violence applies to God's creating activity, which was to deliver the cosmos from formless chaos. In creating life as well as redeeming it, God opposes violence and corruption, and this conflict costs God. It costs life to deliver life from lifelessness, whether that be corruption and violence now or the formless void at the beginning. It is by giving over or imparting life that deliverance from lifelessness is achieved. To deliver from the death of corruption and violence or from a formless void, life must be imparted or bequeathed. It takes an investment of life to liberate life from lifelessness, releasing bound potential so that it can realize its purpose.

These considerations reveal several things. For one, Jesus's crucifixion shows how potent the power of darkness is in the world—and, from what we now know, may end the world. Second, opposing those powers comes with a cost. It takes an expenditure of life to deliver life from lifelessness, whether that be corruption and violence now or from the deep darkness at the beginning. And finally, love can succeed. The love of God manifested in Jesus's life and death and carried on in his communities was undaunted by those powers, unselfish in their love, and proved to be successful over dark powers in the world. Love faced up to opposition, was costly, and worked. This gives hope that love can prevail over destructiveness and deliver us from corruption, encouraging us to take the leap do the same.

When we develop the idea that Jesus's life and death gives us clear insight into what is truly going on in the world, then, the creation, like redemption, was costly. To preserve life in the face of threats, moreover, will be costly for us as well, requiring courage to do so. In the context we have laid out, principled living must be undaunted and unselfish. But that is what creatures, who, from the biblical point of view, are made in the Creator's likeness, are to do.

It should not surprise us, then, that resisting lifelessness to protect life will cost creatures when it cost the Creator to do the same. It should not surprise us that there is a price to be paid to oppose futile existence and for us to realize our purpose in life when there was a price to be paid to deliver the cosmos from chaos so that it could realize its potential. When we live principled lives, we initiate the same general activity that started and upholds the creation itself, instituting rules that support life and oppose lifelessness.

We know that principled living will be costly. There will be misjudgments and failures, even successes will seem ineffectual, and it will be difficult to live that way persistently. But if we do so with the hope that the initiative behind the creation of the universe—driving the evolution that led to beings like us who could love others—was itself loving, then we would be inspired to love that way too. Persistent principled living with the hope that it can prevail over corruption and violence is what love is. For a world in the clutches of lifelessness, actions that free it for life are invaluable.

Taken as a whole, the Bible is the story of the love of God for the world. It is a special kind of love. The Bible is about a love that faces opposition, that costs, that is unselfish, and that is life-giving. It is all those things because it is a love that frees us from bondage so that we in turn freely serve others with a love that frees. Love accounts for love. The Bible claims that God loves the world, freeing it from chaos to realize its potential, creating humanity to do on Earth what God is doing in the universe: freeing from captivity to disorder and corruption in order to realize its purposes. The biblical point of view invites us to draw a parallel between the Creator's view of the universe and the creature's view of the world. The idea that humans are created in the likeness of the Creator suggests that our role in promoting life in the world—like tending the garden in Genesis—is analogous to the Creator's sustaining the universe.

Biblical theology points to these deeper roots in order to account for what we observe aboveground. Or, reversing the image, it appropriates our worldview but overlays it with biblical themes and concepts in order to find a higher congruence, seeing how they can inform and even amplify each other. When we align them in this way, we might see connections that fill in and complete our worldview. Superimposing them, we might see that the biblical worldview provides a larger context in order to think from a wider perspective, allowing us to propose fitting responses to fundamental questions that press for answers. To lay biblical themes and concepts over our worldview in this way involves some extending and contracting. The aim is to see how they can play off of and supplement each other, not to bend either view out of shape. What matters is whether the resulting worldview aligns our three questions in a way that orients our lives and grounds our hope.

We know, to conclude, that the creation is threatened with a return to chaos, the evolution of life challenged by lifelessness, and human life threatened with destruction. The continuation of the universe, we know, cannot be presumed; the initiative that created the universe must continue to drive evolution forward and sustain it in order to prevent its disintegration. In view of these persistent threats to the universe, which we know are powerful enough to destroy the universe, its continuance requires continuing action in order for the universe to be sustained.

As we noted, what drives creation, starting nature on its way, and keeps it on track, preventing it from ending up in simply inert or utterly disordered states, are stable laws providing constancies and harmonies, allowing matter to develop in predictable ways. From these interactions emerge regularities and patterns, forming novel connections between parts and wholes, quickening relationships between them, giving rise to more highly organized structures. Information, as we understand it today, passed within structures, systems, and cells, directing constructive development. In these ways, nature does not remain stuck in static inertness or spin off into endless disorder but continues to move forward—keeping alive, we might say, its potential for life, even while lifelessness threatens. Disinformation, by contrast, as in the case of cancerous cells and mutant genes, leads to fatal results, often to premature death.[5]

In humans, we can see further, matter's potential surged, leapt to become beings who have minds, self-awareness, and wills, and so who can

---

5. See Davies, *Demon in the Machine*.

reason, empathize, and act freely. This was not an accident, and it was not foreordained. It was, rather, because purposive activity formed matter so that it might become this despite chaotic factors at work to suppress it. It makes sense, then, to say that the reason human beings have minds, self-awareness, and wills is because something mindful and willful initiated that development. It requires a leap in our understanding to believe that (in that it goes beyond what we can know) just as, similarly, it is a "quantum leap" in the development of matter to go from brains to minds, feelings to self-consciousness, and instinctual behavior to purposeful conduct (which we also do not yet understand). So also it is a leap to conduct ourselves as ethical beings since it incurs risks and costs. It makes good sense, though, to adopt those convictions and to act that way, for in that way we live up to our potential, actualizing our capacities to protect, preserve, and promote life, thereby opposing threats that press toward lifelessness.

In view of this largely lifeless universe—though one with the potential for living things and intelligent beings—delivering the universe from that state so that it might realize its potential was a purposeful—mindful and willful—act. The deliverance of the world from deep darkness, as well as the deliverance of humanity from corruption and violence, proved costly and must continue. From this point of view, then, initiating the universe was not only purposeful—mindful and willful—but empathetic and loving. It takes love such as that to generate and promote life and to protect and preserve it from lifelessness and brutishness. Opposing this lifeless, formless void, trapped in a state of disorder (but having the potential for living things and intelligent beings), and delivering the universe from that state was an act of love. When we see the creation and evolution of the cosmos as the deliverance from chaos that held the world captive and that continues to threaten it, then, and with an eye toward the biblical story, we see that it was love that initiated the creation, sustains it, and we hope will continue to do so. To look ahead to the next section, we can see that even if the creation comes to nothing, love succeeded.

On this way of thinking, then, love brought the universe into being; it is the originating, the primordial act. Love is the reason that the universe exists at all, that it is protected from futility and kept from descending back into nothingness. Love was in play from the very beginning, made life possible, and brought into existence beings who themselves could oppose lifelessness, protect life, and who could love. Love is the driving force in the life of the universe; and, given that the threats to the world have not ceased, we can have faith that that action is continuing. Hoping that that is so inspires us to do the same: help free others from futile lives so that they can realize their purpose in living.

How then should we answer the question, "Where can we place our hope?" Our hope is in the power of love. Since love initiated the creation, wresting matter from chaos, freeing the universe to realize its potential; and preserves it, advancing the life-giving in defiance of the lifeless; and fulfills its purpose, opposing violence and delivering others from it, then we might hope that that love will prevail over destructiveness in the end. That is biblical faith and hope. Such faith is not knowledge because it accepts uncertainty and acts on its convictions despite that. Such hope also is not wishful thinking but expectant acting. Such love aims not inward, not upward, but outward. Undaunted by deep darkness, it opposes it, choosing the harder, narrower way, not the easier, wider way. Taking the leap to live that way, love fulfills the purpose of life, as we will see in the final section.

LEAP TO LOVE

"In everything do to others as you would have them do to you; for this is the law and the prophets" (Matt 7:12). "For the whole law is summed up in a single commandment, 'You shall love your neighbor as yourself'" (Gal 5:14). That is how the Bible, as well as many religions and philosophies, claims we are to live. The right faith and the proper hope authorize such love, making it the natural thing to do. Seeing our lives within a compelling worldview motivates us to live that way, making it so obvious, so intrinsically the right thing to do, that all other motivations—typically self-serving—fall away. That happens when faith, hope, and love are in concert. That is how biblical theology is supposed to work.

Does it work that way? Or is the call to love others heard as a burden, an unwelcome, troublesome burden, and so goes unanswered? Is it something I avoid doing, do so reluctantly, resentfully, or only after pleas and promises, finding excuses not to, regarding the call as an illegitimate hardship imposed on me? It's not supposed to be that way. Something has gone wrong with biblical theology when love does not spring naturally and spontaneously from faith and hope but requires continual threats and enticements, nagging us to do the right thing. When we do not see intrinsic reasons for living that way and do it for its own sake, we require other motivations to push us to do it. Then those self-serving motives—divine favor, eternal life, guilt avoidance, public recognition—become the real reasons for following the golden rule. And, if I can obtain those things more easily than the costly way of following it—which may never get me those things anyway—I will, because those benefits matter most to me.

It is difficult to harmonize our understanding of faith, hope, and love, as the history of biblical theology shows. It is difficult for readers of the Bible today because our understanding of faith, hope, and love often functions to support and deepen self-serving interests. If we think that faith promises happiness in this life and eternal life in heaven, as is common today, our original self-centeredness is not overcome but reinforced, and unbidden love for others cannot spring free of it. "Love your neighbor as yourself," in that case, will always be a troublesome demand requiring pleading and cajoling, threatening and rewarding.

The reason it is so hard to get us to love others, as we discussed in Part Two, is because it is easier to deny our moral nature, with its natural turn to others, and to remain stuck on ourselves. When we are turned in upon ourselves, preferring to think of ourselves as angels-in-waiting—for whom morality is a secondary concern—or just animals—for which morality does not apply—it is difficult to get us to turn outward, to others. The claim that we are turned in upon ourselves has been constant in biblical theology. The challenge is to align what we can know, what we should do, and what we might hope for in a way that overcomes our original self-centeredness and turns us outside of ourselves to see what is truly going on in the world so that the leap to love others is the natural thing to do.

As we have noted throughout, when faith, hope, and love are not in concert, believers often turn more tightly within themselves, uninspired and unmoved to reach out to others. When faith and hope are misconceived or misguided, love does not follow. If our hope is directed to a *future* life, we will not be moved to love others in *this* life. And if our faith depends on *divine* interventions, not the certainty that our knowledge and actions can better the lives of others—and that it is our purpose in life to do this—*we* will not be emboldened to intervene for them. Love for others does not spring forth naturally from faith and hope when my real hope is for my own happiness in this life or in some hereafter. And when my faith depends upon a supreme being to intercede in nature or society or in my personal life, my motivation to intervene for others wanes.

Believers throughout the ages, of course, have confessed that "God is love" (1 John 4:8, 16), that God loves us, and that we likewise are to love others. Other, misguided ideas, though, get in the way of that clear progression from faith to action. For example, when God is also viewed as a law giver and judge who rewards and punishes compliance and noncompliance with his laws in this world and the next, it is difficult to believe that God is love. It is easy, in that case, to see how fear rather than love pervades biblical theology. When that is the case, the motivation to love others rests upon self-interest. Unselfish love of neighbor will not burst forth.

Today, though, it is more common to think of God not as a judge but as a loving parent who does not punish but who forgives our moral failings unconditionally. The motivation to love in that case is not fear of punishment but gratitude for God's love. In that case, it is not fear that pervades theology, creating an obstacle for faith active in love, but complacency. Because my heavenly Parent will love me regardless of what I do or don't do, my moral acts diminish in importance. The importance of my relationship with my heavenly Parent eclipses my relationship with others. I know that God will overlook my failings in what I have done and left undone—and so I will too. Consequently, I have no intrinsic reason to help my neighbor— certainly not to make up for the damage I have done—and complacency and quietism result.

Problems such as these arise when biblical theology links the good or ill that befall me to my moral action or inaction and places an all-seeing God in charge who appraises them and imposes consequences for them. If personal salvation is the ultimate concern, moreover, as it is for many today, this problem is heightened because then, if my salvation depends on my moral acts, I will be troubled with the problem of works righteousness and have an anxious conscience. ("How can I be sure I have done enough to be saved and have pleased my Father in heaven?") Or, if I will be saved simply if I believe, I will be lulled into quietism and a complacent conscience. ("I am saved by faith alone; God will overlook my moral action and inaction; therefore, what I do and don't do in this world doesn't ultimately matter.") These beliefs are common today; they leave us with a confused worldview, and they cannot warrant the love biblical theology exhorts us to.

These beliefs shackle our reasoning, confuse our self-understanding, and weaken our moral will. They shackle our reasoning by glossing over natural doubts, making us credulous. ("Am I supposed to believe that God is intervening in my life right now? How can I tell where he is or isn't? Is what is happening to me God's will?") They confuse our self-understanding by disorienting and undermining our own experience. ("Is it true that God will always comfort me and guide me? What if I don't experience that? Am I doing something wrong?") They weaken our willpower by ignoring our moral qualms. ("Must I believe that God allows these bad things? Must I accept that they are really for good?")

In an earlier day, when the goal of life was to avoid hell and reach heaven, Christians were terrified with uncertainty over their relationship with their heavenly Father. They could never be sure whether their prayers and practices were adequate or whether their moral lives measured up. Wanting to please God, believers became bargainers with God: if I do this, maybe God will do that. It is easy to see how such misguided religious thinking—more concerned with saving their own souls than helping their neighbor, with their own immortality than the mortal lives of others, with obtaining the next life rather than improving this one—misconstrued their relationship with God as well as others.

Even though few worry about going to hell today and many are sure of God's love, is the fundamental relationship to God, whether divine Judge or heavenly Parent, so different? That is to say, in both cases, God is the supreme being, one to whom we cannot help but implore for help. Since my life or death, my wellbeing or woe are in God's hands, I will want to get good with God. If God is the one in charge, I want to know what my standing is. I will think that without God's favor things may go badly for me. God might withdraw protection from me, even adversely affect my life, and so I will do what I can to stay in God's good graces. I may say, do, or promise anything to be on God's good side and to protect my life. I will want to know: what does God want from me? Inevitably I will find myself in a relationship based on credits and debits—not to avoid hell anymore since few really think they could end up in such a place—but for good or ill in this life. Because I think God can make my life better or withhold his protection and allow it to be worse, I will do what I can to obtain his favor.

If God is my all-knowing heavenly Parent, to elaborate, I will think that my every thought, word, and deed are under God's watchful eye, subject to divine approval or disapproval. (Caption on a church billboard: "'I saw that'—God.") Have I made God happy or sad? Dismayed or jubilant, proud or distraught, amused or unimpressed, calmed or concerned? If God has perfect insight into souls, all these worries and more are in play. As I survey the ups and downs and highs and lows of my life, I will try to discern how God is responding to all that I have done and left undone. I will become very ingenious in interpreting God's attitudes toward me: *this* means that God is happy, or disappointed, or concerned, or trying to coax or to change me, or giving me a final warning; *that* means that I've come around, that God understands, is relieved, etc., etc. But how can I tell? How can I be sure that I am not deceiving myself? Such uncertainty can leave me anxious and conflicted—a troubled soul of the sort that afflicted earlier Christians who worried whether their deeds merited or failed to merit God's favor. If nothing else, such uncertainty tempts me to fool myself, flatter my own wishes, and bless my own desires as "what God wants for me."

This predicament will consume my attention, distract me from doing what I can to improve life, and leave me in an anxious state, much as it did to Luther who agonized over finding favor with God and who was mortified by the prospect of God's judgment. The objectives are different now—protection from troubles in this life, not the horrors of hell—but the predicament is the same: what does God want from me, and how can I tell? I tie myself into knots when I think of an all-powerful person watching over the world and acting in my life. I will continually monitor my relationship with God, scrutinizing all my experiences: now God is warning me, now God is encouraging me, now guiding, now chastening. It becomes an all-absorbing, equivocal, unending, and ultimately futile quest to track the course of my life, one where I continually take my spiritual pulse, wondering what this or that experience means for my relationship with God. It can become a personal obsession that works against active love for others—the hallmark of the Christian life—because it turns us inward, not outward. Whether the objective is to avoid punishment in the hereafter or to obtain protection in this life, the effort to negotiate with and to gain favor with God is the same. The same view of God we challenged above—that God can intervene in nature and history, suspending natural laws and historical patterns—now invades our personal lives: a supreme being who can do whatever he wants, who may or may not reveal his will to us, who may or may not keep us from harm, who may or may not bring us happiness—whatever his inscrutable will happens to be.

Even though we begin from a different starting point than five hundred years ago, we wind up in the same place. If I begin with the belief that God is a supreme being who intervenes in my personal world, I will think that God can do the same thing in my natural and social worlds: change the course of natural processes and intervene in social circumstances—the same misunderstanding discussed above. This worry will always be present: maybe if I did more, prayed more, or trusted God more, God will protect me more.

It is no longer a constructive belief to think that God will suspend the laws of nature and miraculously intervene in the world. It misconceives the way God relates to natural and human life. Similarly, when we think that prayers to God and pledges to trust in him lead to favorable circumstances, we misconceive the way God acts in our personal lives. There are constructive ways to understand the power of prayer and worship, but this is not one of them. The true exercise of faith, this essay has argued, is the one put to us by the moral challenges before us, by what we do to help others. How we measure up to them is the best test, something all can see—not simply imagined by me or known only by God—and the best way to weigh faithfulness. And when we do that, ironically, self-forgetting is the result. I no longer obsess over my own faithfulness.

When our understandings of faith and hope are misguided, our understanding of what love is will be skewed as well. When biblical theology does not properly align faith and hope, love will not spring spontaneously from them. How, then, should we understand what love is given our understanding of faith and hope? "Love" is an overused and trivialized word. To capture its true power today, we have to distinguish it from misleading meanings it has come to have and view it from the biblical perspective proposed.

Given the preceding discussion, to love is not simply to have good feelings or thoughts for another. It is not simply accepting others or desiring what is best for them. It is not simply showing them acts of kindness. In all these cases, "love" can mean merely having affection or signaling favor, requiring nothing from us. The love we are pointing toward differs from romantic, filial, or familial love, and it is different from what believers often understand by "agape" love. In light of the preceding discussion, what does love mean, and why can we say it works? What is love from this biblical perspective? Given our circumstances, love operates in a world where corruption and violence can spin out of control, threatening civilization and all life. When life is under threat in the way we have described, we can see that love faces perils, and that it must set itself against corruption and destruction if it is to preserve life and protect the dignity of human life.

When love confronts such opposition, to begin with, we no longer see love primarily as a relationship between two persons, as we typically do. Love is not simply a personal interaction. Love, rather, is set against threats to life that must be opposed, and concerns itself with what must be done to oppose them. Because love occurs in the face of opposition, to put it another way, love is not simply a paired or dual phenomenon. To understand love aright we must take into account this third element, the undercurrent of corruption and destruction that threatens to pull us into lifelessness. To love, then, in this understanding, is to give help, unselfishly and dearly, to free others from those things that threaten their lives.

Because love faces real opposition, accordingly, it must be courageous; and because it aims to free us for responsible life in the face of that opposition, it must be principled. Understood in this way, love frees *from* those things that keep us from living out our humanity and *for* fulfilling our humanity. In that way, love frees from lifelessness, from bondage to futile existence. Loving others frees them from that which enslaves them, freeing them in turn to help others be free from their own enslavements, as we discussed in the last section.

To describe this more completely, we realize our own freedom when we set others free. My freedom is not in attaining personal objectives such as self-realization. Self-realization occurs, instead, when I use my freedom to free others. We fulfill our human nature as free beings when we use our capabilities to free others from things that lead to futile lives—so that they are free to free others, and so on. Authentic freedom is compelled to free others so that they, in turn, do the same. When we live that way we realize the purpose of human life. To put it paradoxically, true freedom is a form of bondage that binds us to others. Then we are "completely free of everything" and "completely attentive to the needs of all," as Luther put it. That is our triumph over the powers of lifelessness that hold us captive.[6]

Acting to free others from that which keeps them from living out their full humanity is life's aim. Love frees bodies, minds, and wills from the deprivations, compulsions, and preoccupations that ensnare them, limiting their lives and degrading their worth. Love fuses freedom and service. Love transforms the lives of those who are touched by it, of course; but it also turns around those who reach out to others because the effect of loving others is to free from self-love.

Nothing uplifts and inspires us as much as witnessing loving acts. We admire them, and, were it not for anxieties and fears that often paralyze us, are moved to do the same. They are incandescent examples of what is possible for us. When we see what love does, we are moved to "go and do likewise." We have all witnessed such acts, we have all been beneficiaries of them, and, most notably, we have all done them. A proper worldview—one that sees what is going on in the world and what we can do in it, and one that gives us hope that love is at the heart of the universe—draws us to leap into love. When acting that way becomes routine and a matter of course, furthermore, loves becomes self-forgetting.

The imperative to love others takes us outside of ourselves, and ultimate concern for ourselves recedes. The primary question no longer is "What about me?" or "What will happen to me?" but "What is really going on in the world and how can I be part of it?" That can't happen when we are captive to the worldview that the goal of life is to be happy—looking past the needs of those around me—or that we are immortals—looking past our life on Earth. Our consuming interest in preserving our own lives and in increasing our own happiness recede when the enormity and importance of what is going on in the world grasps us. Then the sights unfolding before our eyes, revealing what is real, stir us into action and override the voices in our heads lulling us into complacency.

Such love, then, is not familial, fraternal, or romantic love, though there is a resemblance among them. It is, rather, a love for others *in general*, a love for all who exist in the same world, not directed specifically to family, friends, or lovers. It is not based on attraction, desire, or friendship. It is not the reaction to a command, or done out of gratitude, or for personal

---

6. That is the way Luther described the freedom of Christian life. Lull and Russell, *Theological Writings*, 404.

merit. It is not done because self-sacrifice is good for the soul, or because self-abasement is an ideal, or martyrdom a goal.

Christian Scriptures call such love, God's love, "agape love," and we usually think that it is most similar to parental love. This similarity, however, has limitations, as we noted above. The principal shortcoming is that we never get beyond thinking of ourselves as children, children who always fall short and who continually need comforting. For God's children, God's word always ends up being, "There, there, everything will be all right." Rather than the love of a parent, it would be better to see the love of God as the love a leader has for disciples. It is the love the head of a mission has for followers united in a cause for which the leader is willing to risk their life. For disciples, accordingly, God's word is always, "Follow me," and "Love one another as I have loved you." From the biblical point of view, God is going out ahead into the world with the aim of setting captives free, enlisting followers into that mission. The kind of love at issue is closer to the love of comrades in arms, of fellow workers sharing a common commitment to oppose corruption and destructiveness and to advance human dignity. Love like that joins us in a common cause against powers threatening to wreak havoc in the world.

Sometimes we say that such love is "self-less." That, too, is misleading if it means "heedless." Such love challenges us to set aside our wishes, but not to be careless, since sustaining ourselves is vital for responding to the challenges before us. It takes courage to take the leap to love others, but it is not a suicidal plunge. I am no good to others if I destroy myself. Assessing our own effectiveness, or being self-critical, is necessary if we are to meet the needs of others. Such love leads us to be "wise as serpents and innocent as doves" (Matt 10:16), not reckless or foolhardy. So it is better to say that such love is "unselfish" rather than "self-less."

Or, sometimes we say that such love is "self-sacrificing." That also is misleading. It is better to say "unself-conscious" or "self-forgetting." If I say I am "self-sacrificing," I am centered on myself, self-consciously focusing on my own suffering, or loss, or the effects of my acts on myself. I need to be self-critical in order to be effective for others, as we just noted; but that does not mean self-focused, where I constantly take my pulse, measure my feelings, and appraise my own worth. "Self-sacrificing" is inward looking, too keen to measure and remember personal costs. If I claim that my love is self-sacrificing, more than likely I will see it as a means for achieving an end other than the love of neighbor, that end being my own worthiness and the satisfaction that gives me or God. The love we are describing, rather, is not "self-sacrificing" but "self-forgetting" because it is turned outward to others, not turned inward to one's own feelings or costs to oneself.

Or, we might think that such love is the response to God's love, or gratitude. That may have been true in an earlier day but is less so now. That was true when I believed that God gave his only Son's life to save me from damnation; then, out of gratitude for being saved from hell, I could be moved to give my life for others as God gave his Son's life for me. But now, since few think they will end up in hell, there is no need for God to save us from it, so we can hardly be grateful for deliverance from something we don't believe exits or will happen. Second, few of us in first-world countries see life as a gift to be grateful for to the degree the love described envisions. We take life for granted, and our expectations go far beyond life itself, to happiness and self-fulfillment. Gratitude simply for being alive is not motivator enough to turn us outside of ourselves toward others in love. The centripetal force of self-love is too strong. Gratitude for my life may spark feelings of affection for my family and friends, but it is not enough to fire love for neighbor, let alone strangers. Even if my heart feels "I should be grateful for my blessings," my head thinks, "Yes, and just because God wants me to count my blessings, God wants to spare me from 'unblessings' or life's hardships." Besides that, we think the comfort that comes from a personal relationship with God is too important to be troubled by the hardships that come from fraught relationships with others.

While I might think, then, that gratitude for life's blessings will spur me to respond to the needs of others, in practice it doesn't. Why? It is *just because* I like my life and all I have; so much so, I do not want to part with any of it, because that would make me *less* content, and I would feel *less* grateful. Towards the end of my life I may well look back with a feeling of largesse and want to "give back"; but when I'm in the middle of it, I find it hard to part with all the things I have been blessed with. If I see myself as a vessel that has been filled I may feel grateful; but then any depletion is a deficit, *less* to be thankful for. The bounteousness of my life cannot be the source of my gratitude, then, because when the bounty diminishes, as it inevitably will, I will have less to be thankful for. From the biblical point of view, moreover, it is not enough to say that life is a "gift from God" to be grateful for, but that "life is God's" to be lived for the love of God. And that gets at the heart of the misunderstanding: as long as I look at life as *mine*, and all my assets as *mine*, the needs of others will never get a fair hearing. Gratitude looks inward, focused on what it has; love looks outward, toward what the world needs. Gratitude looks inward to count *my* blessings; it does not look outward to innumerate the needs, shortcomings, hardships, and afflictions—or "unblessings"—of others.

A biblical worldview turns the focus from myself to others, turning the centripetal force of self-love outward to the needs of others. Whereas gratitude gazes at myself and what I have, love sees what is really going on in the world and what it needs. It understands what needs to be done to protect life—to resist the evils in the world and to promote human dignity. Faith recognizes that it is not enough to say, "My life is a gift from God"—that would be gratitude—but that "Life is God's"—which turns me outside of myself to do what I can for the lives of others—that is love. Then we see ourselves not as vessels who are full, parting with some of what we have that we can spare, but conduits, vehicles for responding to the needs of the world. Gratitude is better understood as the spontaneity that springs from being grasped by the needs of the world and the realization that we have a part to play in meeting them.

When we are invested in the moral tasks before us, as we are when we have hope that love is working through the world to overcome corruption and destructiveness, then self-love recedes, and love for others takes its place. I turn inward just to size up and assess what I can do to contribute to the world. Then my internal focus is essentially self-critical in order better to focus my concern outside myself. My self-love, in other words, is turned inside out.

LOVE WORKS

Love as we have described it, then, is spontaneous, unselfish, and self-forgetting. It is spontaneous in that it sees what needs to be done without pausing to calculate "What's in it for me?" It is unselfish in that it does what is there for it to do, measuring its effects on others, not oneself. It is self-forgetting because it loses memory of its good deeds. The more our moral capacities are turned outward, the more the needs of others will silence the wants and desires making noise inside us; the more often we take that leap, the more those capacities will be strengthened; and the more we overcome the compulsion to turn inward, the more self-concern will fade away.

Gerhard Forde recalled a story about a pastor on her deathbed. Anxious friends asked her whether she knew she would be saved. She said she was. They asked, "how can you be so sure?" She replied that it was because she could not recall having done a good deed in her life. That is the way spontaneous, unselfish, self-forgetting faith active in love works.

Freedom from slavery, we discussed in the last section, is a movement central to the biblical story. It is also one of the drivers of human history, it describes the trajectory of many lives, and it is a dynamic that may help us understand the course of the universe as a whole, of where it came from and where it is going. The point of the creation, we can see, was to deliver reality from futile existence so that it could realize its potential. In the biblical world, deliverance meant freedom from idolatry, from physical servitude, as well as from political and religious tyranny, all so that the people of Israel could live according to God's law, as God intended. For people living today in the first world, deliverance can mean freedom from materialism, consumerism, militarism, oppressive social relationships, psychological addictions and emotional burdens, as well as self-inflicted indulgences. All those things can enslave us in that they make us insensitive to life's true purposes, indifferent to others, and unwilling to reach out to them, let alone act out of love.

We can draw a parallel, then, between the threats the universe and our own world are under, between a God's eye or macro view and our own micro view. In both cases, we can describe those circumstances as enslavement to lifeless forces that can lead to the disintegration of the universe and to the destruction of life on Earth. We can explain the creation of the universe in those terms, seeing the creation as an incursion to free reality from chaos so that it could realize its potential. And we can account for the protection and promotion of life on Earth in similar terms. We can, furthermore, draw the parallel that just as it cost the Creator to give life to the creation, so also there is a cost to preserve life on Earth and to free bound human potential.

We know, however, that these parallel lines could come to an end, that the universe might disintegrate and return to a formless void. Its potential might not continue to develop but dissipate into useless energy. We also know, before that happens, that living systems could plunge into a state of permanent lifelessness, and human beings might succumb to corruption and violence, ending civilized life. If the cosmos descends into chaos in these ways, does that mean the creation was pointless? To put it directly, did God fail? What good is love, we might ask, if that is how it all ends?

The answer to these questions is that the deliverance of the cosmos from chaos succeeded because life and love existed. Life emerged from lifelessness, and love arose to protect and promote life. That's all we need to see. The purpose of the creation and of human existence is to free from lifelessness. This purpose, the aim of the creation, and life's fulfillment has been realized even though the world returns to nothing.

If the universe is to disintegrate, abolishing any hope for its future, what should we conclude? First of all, hope for this world need not be the expectation that it will continue forever. Hope resides, rather, in what the world can become. At issue is not whether the world will endure forever but what becomes of it, whether matter came to actualize its potential, whether it overcame lifelessness. In the case of human life, freeing others from bondage so that they can, in turn, free others, is of greater value than the mere continuous existence of life.

For us, love is life's end in itself, whether or not life continues. Whether or not the universe continues to exist, where there is love, the universe has realized its purpose. When that happens, the purpose of the creation is fulfilled. In the Gospel according to John, in a similar way, eternal life is not, in the first place, endless life, but a qualitative state of living in this life. Eternal life can exist now, according to that Gospel. Similarly, hope for this world is not in its endlessness but that it realizes its purpose. When that happens, we might say hope "takes care of itself," and the future is no longer an open question because it is realized in the present. To love is to live in a state where the future is drawn into the present, and so is fulfilled, to put it abstractly. The gospel message is that where there is love, life is fulfilled, even if life is no more.

The goal of creation is not to start lives that will never end but to bring about love in lives that will end. The goal is not to begin lives that will exist forever but lives that end in—realize their purpose in—freeing others from lifelessness. What matters is that love existed, not that life exists forever. In the Hebrew Bible we read, "Love is strong as death" (Song 8:6). In light of Jesus's life and the life of communities founded in his name, the Christian Scriptures witness that love is stronger than death. That is the central concept in the resurrection: death does not cancel love, because it is stronger than death. With love life defeats death. The purpose of the creation is realized when love arises and overcomes lifelessness.

Such love is courageous and costly. It is a risk but worth it because the emergence of love is more valuable than life itself. It is worth it because potential, captive to futility, prevented from actualizing its potential, is a scourge upon existence, just as human captivity is a plague upon humanity. It was worth it to deliver the universe from purposeless existence, even if it cost the Creator; and deliverance from enslavements is gain even if it costs us.

As we discussed in a previous section, there is a death that is worse than death. Death, understood as corruption or degradation, can be worse than death understood as the end of life. Enslavement is a case in point. Because human life has dignity, to abuse and subjugate bodies, minds, and wills can be worse than ending human life. Enslavement degrades humanity and thereby shows contempt for humanity. This is true both for the enslaved as well as the enslavers, for those who corrupt their own human capabilities by using them to degrade the humanity in others. Slavery, consequently, wrongs all of us.

Death, understood both as the corruption of life and the end of life, is elucidated by Paul when he wrote "the wages of sin is death" (Rom 6:23), "sin exercised dominion in death" (5:21), and "sin, working death in me" (7:13). Käsemann comments on Paul's perspective, "Precisely in our acts we are exponents of a power which transforms the cosmos into chaos."[7] Slavery, self-evidently, is a form of death in that sense, as, in lesser degrees, are enslavements to all those things that misuse and abuse our bodies, minds, and wills.

Because human life has dignity it is worthy of respect, and we are to use human life to uphold that dignity and to show that respect, even if it endangers life, the lives of both those who must be freed, and those who endeavor to free them, both the enslaved and the liberators. Because the corruption and degradation of life can be worse than the end of life, it is worth it to expend life—risk natural death—in order to dignify life—oppose the corruption and degradation of life, or death.

Slavery provokes moral revulsion in us, and it is a wrong that must be righted. That was not generally the case two hundred years ago, and it is a sign of moral progress that we view slavery that way today. We might confirm this if we imagine that we came upon an enslaved people, toiling for slavers who subjugate them against their will and for their own gain. Suppose further that it is in our power—though not without risk to our own lives—to free them. Would we feel bound to help them? Of course we would. We would try to gain their freedom even if it cost us. Imagine, next, that we mount an insurgency to free them. The slaves rise up against their enslavers, overthrow them, and escape to freedom. The insurrection, however, fails to free all the slaves and does not last; many are killed, many are recaptured and returned to slavery, and only some are freed. Setting aside other considerations—the particulars of the enslavement, the number freed and killed, etc.—was the deliverance, albeit short-lived and limited, worth it? Yes. Did it fail? No. Why? Because the value of being freed from slavery is invaluable. Slavery thwarted—even for a time, even if emancipation is not made complete—is better than no freedom at all.

Freeing the enslaved from the grip of slavery rarely happens without courage and a costly fight, as was the case in the American Civil War. Many felt compelled to join that fight at great risk, even if it cost them their lives. To a lesser degree, wresting social, economic, and political power from those who use it to dominate others almost always requires sacrificing something of value. There are, additionally, many other kinds of powers that hold minds, souls, and wills in bondage. To rescue minds from ignorance and superstition, souls from addictions and compulsions, and wills from cowardice and complacency requires risk and cost. We rightly feel obligated to do what we can to help, and most of us will—and have. A good measure of the value of freedom from such enslavements is that those who

---

7. Käsemann, *Commentary on Romans*, 154.

are freed—who know what enslavement is—also know the imperative to do what they can to help those subjugated by it.

The reason the cosmos exists was to free matter from enslavement so that it could realize its potential, the apex of which is beings who can, in turn, free others from all that enslaves them. That alone is triumph over chaos, even if the cosmos ceases to be. The end or goal of the creation can be realized even if the universe is no more.

Biblical faith is that God opposed the chaos holding reality in its grip. We, too, can be insurgents who oppose lifelessness and promote life. Biblical faith is that love initiated the creation, brought something from nothing, generated life, and developed beings who could love. Even if this does not continue, even if chaos is not finally subdued and brought into the orbit of love, love did not fail. When we have faith that love is the law of life—that love initiated life and that love is the way to respond to threats to life—we will do likewise. We will take the leap when we believe that love is the power animating the universe, hoping that the universe itself will be saved from the powers that threaten it with destruction.

Love delivers from enslavements, freeing the enslaved for purposeful existence. In that way we can say God is love, as the biblical tradition commonly has. God is love as we have described it: the freeing from powers that keep existence in bondage so that it can realize its purpose, which, for us, is to protect life and love others. Even if we fall short in this, as it appeared Jesus did, and even if the universe should return to nothingness, as many forecast, God succeeded in bringing life to the universe, and we succeeded in defying lifelessness. Love throttles lifelessness and gives life a chance. That is invaluable, even if life comes to nothing in the end. Love gives existence meaning even if the universe disintegrates and is no more. Why? Because it defied the chaos that held existence in bondage and enabled it to realize what it could be.

It was better to defy and challenge the deep darkness than to leave reality a formless void; better that matter was freed from futile existence than that its potential remained bound; better that love came to be than that it did not. It is better to try to realize potential—even if not completely—than to leave potential forever trapped and chaos unchallenged. The cosmos that came into being has value, unlike the chaos at the beginning. It was better that the universe came to be—came free from chaos—so that it could be free to realize its potential—even if it comes to be no more—than that reality remained forever a formless void.

Bibliography

Barth, Karl. *Church Dogmatics*. Edinburgh: T. & T. Clark, 1961.
Bonting, Sjoerd, L. *Chaos Theology: A Revised Creation Theology*. Ottawa: Novalis, 2002.
Boyd, Gregory A. "Evolution as Cosmic Warfare: A Biblical Perspective on Satan and 'Natural Evil.'" In *Creation Made Free: An Open Theology Engaging Science*, edited by Thomas Jay Ord, 125–47. Eugene, OR: Pickwick, 2009.
———. *God at War: The Bible and Spiritual Conflict*. Downers Grove, IL: InterVarsity, 1997.
Caputo, John D. *Cross and Cosmos*. Bloomington: Indiana University Press, 2019.
Clayton, Philip, and Paul Davies, eds. *The Re-Emergence of Emergence*. Oxford: Oxford University Press, 2006.
Dalai Lama [Tenzin Gyatso]. *The Universe in a Single Atom: The Convergence of Science and Spirituality*. New York: Random House, 2005.
Davies, Paul. *The Demon in the Machine: How Hidden Webs of Information Are Solving the Mystery of Life*. London: Penguin, 2019.
———. *Templeton Prize Address*. Nassau: Lismore, 1995.
———. *What's Eating the Universe?* Chicago: University of Chicago Press, 2021.
Dembski, William. *The End of Christianity: Finding a Good God in an Evil World*. Nashville: B. & H., 2009.
Dennett, Daniel. *Consciousness Explained*. Boston: Little, Brown, 1991.
Doudna, Jennifer A., and Samuel H. Sternberg. *A Crack in Creation: Gene Editing and the Unthinkable Power to Control Evolution*. New York: Houghton Mifflin Harcourt, 2017.
Douglass, Frederick. "Narrative of the Life of Frederick Douglass, an American Slave." In *Narrative of the Life of Frederick Douglass, an American Slave & Incidents in the Life of a Slave Girl*, 1–114. Modern Library Classics. New York: Modern Library, 2000.
Dyson, Freeman. *Infinite in All Directions*. New York: Harper & Row, 1988.
Frank, Adam. "The Day Before Genesis." *Discover* 29.4 (2008) 54–60.
Green, Ronald M. "Kant on Christian Love." In *The Love Commandments: Essays in Christian Ethics and Moral Philosophy*, edited by Edmund N. Santurri. Georgetown: Georgetown University Press, 1992.
Guyer, Paul. *Kant*. London: Routledge, 2006.
Halpern, Paul. *The Allure of the Multiverse: Extra Dimensions, Other Worlds, and Parallel Universes*. New York: Basic, 2024.
Haught, John. *Christianity and Science*. Maryknoll: Orbis, 2007.

———. *God After Darwin: A Theology of Evolution*. London: Routledge, 2007.
———. "Science, God, and Cosmic Purpose." *The Cambridge Companion to Science and Religion*, edited by Peter Harrison, 261–62. Cambridge: Cambridge University Press, 2010.
Hawking, Stephen. *A Brief History of Time*. London: Bantam, 1988.
Hawking, Stephen, and Leonard Mlodinow. *The Grand Design*. New York: Bantam, 2010.
Heisenberg, Werner. *Philosophy and Physics: The Revolution in Modern Science*. New York: Harper & Row, 1958.
Jacobs, Harriet. "Incidents in the Life of a Slave Girl." In *Narrative of the Life of Frederick Douglass, an American Slave & Incidents in the Life of a Slave Girl*, 115–354. Modern Library Classics. New York: Modern Library, 2000.
Kaku, Michio. *The Future of Humanity: Our Destiny in the Universe*. New York: Anchor, 2018.
Kant, Immanuel. *The Critique of Judgement*. Translated by J. C. Meredith. Oxford: Oxford University Press, 1952.
Käsemann, Ernst. *Commentary on Romans*. Translated and edited by Geoffrey W. Bromiley. Grand Rapids: Eerdmans, 1980.
Kaufman, Stuart. *A World Beyond Physics: The Emergence and Evolution of Life*. Oxford: Oxford University Press, 2019.
Keller, Catherine. *Face of the Deep: A Theology of Becoming*. New York: Routledge, 2003.
Levinson, Jon. *Creation and the Persistence of Evil: The Jewish Drama of Divine Omnipotence*. Princeton: Princeton University Press, 1998.
Lewis, C. S. *Mere Christianity*. New York: Macmillan, 1943.
Lincoln, Bruce. *Gods and Demons, Priests and Scholars*. Chicago: University of Chicago Press, 2012.
Lull, Timothy F., and William R. Russell, eds. *Martin Luther's Basic Theological Writings*. Minneapolis: Fortress, 2012.
Luther, Martin. "A Mighty Fortress Is Our God." *Lutheran Book of Worship*, 228. Minneapolis: Lutheran Church in America, 1978.
MacAskill, William. *What We Owe the Future: A Million-Year View*. London: Oneworld, 2022.
May, Gerhard. *Creatio Ex Nihilo: The Doctrine of "Creation out of Nothing" in Early Christian Thought*. Translated by A. S. Worrall. Edinburgh: T. & T. Clark, 1994.
Messer, Neil. "Evolution and Theodicy: How (Not) to Do Science and Theology." *Zygon* 53.3 (2018) 821–35.
Miller, Kenneth R. *Finding Darwin's God: A Scientist's Search for Common Ground Between God and Evolution*. New York: Harper, 2007.
Nagel, Thomas. *Mind and Cosmos: Why the Materialist Neo-Darwinian Conception of Nature Is Almost Certainly False*. Oxford: Oxford University Press, 2012.
Ord, Thomas Jay. "An Open Theology Doctrine of Creation and the Solution to the Problem of Evil." In *Creation Made Free: An Open Theology Engaging Science*, edited by Thomas Jay Ord, 28–51. Eugene, OR: Pickwick, 2009.
Ord, Toby. *The Precipice: Existential Risk and the Future of Humanity*. New York: Hachette, 2020.
Pannenberg, Wolfhart. *Systematic Theology*. Grand Rapids: Eerdmans, 1998.
Peters, Ted. *God as Trinity*. Louisville: Westminster John Knox, 1993.

Polkinghorne, John. *Exploring Reality: The Intertwining of Science and Religion.* New Haven, CT: Yale University Press, 2005.
———. *The God of Hope and the End of the World.* London: SPCK, 2002.
———. *Science and Religion in Quest of the Truth.* New Haven, CT: Yale University Press, 2011.
Rosen, Jeffrey. *The Pursuit of Happiness: How Classical Writers on Virtue Inspired the Lives of the Founders and Defined America.* New York: Simon & Schuster, 2024.
Rosen, Michael. *Dignity: Its Meaning and History.* Cambridge: Harvard University Press, 2012.
Rupp, E. Gordon, and Philip S. Watson, eds. *Luther and Erasmus: Free Will and Salvation.* Philadelphia: Westminster, 1969.
Russell, R. J. *Cosmology: from Alpha to Omega.* Minneapolis: Fortress, 2008.
Sollereder, Bethany. *God, Evolution, and Animal Suffering: Theodicy Without a Fall.* New York: Routledge, 2019.
Southgate, Christopher. *God, Humanity, and the Cosmos.* London: T. & T. Clark, 1999.
———. "Response with a Select Bibliography." *Zygon* 53.3 (2018) 909–30.
Steinhardt, Paul J., and Neil Turok. *Endless Universe: Beyond the Big Bang.* New York: Random House, 2007.
Tanner, Kathryn. "Eschatology Without a Future?" In *The End of the World and the Ends of God*, edited by John Polkinghorne and Michael Welker, 222–37. Harrisburg: Trinity, 2002.
Teilhard de Chardin, Pierre. *How I Believe.* New York: Harper & Row, 1969.
Torrance, T. F. *The Christian Doctrine of God: One Being, Three Persons.* Edinburgh: T. & T. Clark, 1996.
Trigg, Roger. *Beyond Matter: Why Science Needs Metaphysics.* West Conshohocken, PA: Templeton, 2015.
Tsumura, David. *Creation and Destruction: A Reappraisal of the* Chaoskampf *Theory in the Old Testament.* Winona Lake, IN: Eisenbrauns, 2005.
Watson, Rebecca S. *Chaos Uncreated: A Reassessment of the Theme of "Chaos" in the Hebrew Bible.* Berlin: Walter de Gruyter, 2005.
Westermann, Claus. *Isaiah 40–66.* London: SCM, 1969.
Wilkinson, David. *Christian Eschatology and the Physical Universe.* London: T. & T. Clark, 2010.
Wisnefske, Ned. *Could God Fail? The Fate of the Universe and the Faith of Christians.* Eugene, OR: Cascade, 2020.
———. *God Hides: A Critique of Religion and a Primer for Faith.* Eugene, OR: Pickwick, 2010.
Worthing, Mark William. *God, Creation, and Contemporary Physics.* Minneapolis: Fortress, 1996.
Zorthian, Julia. "Stephen Hawking Says Humans Have 100 Years to Move to Another Planet." *Time*, May 4, 2017. https://time.com/4767595/stephen-hawking-100-years-new-planet/.

Index

actions
    of God, 45, 47
    and happiness, 55
Adam, 35, 38, 39, 86
affection, 98
afterlife, 6, 34
agape, 95, 97
American Civil War, 102
annihilation
    vs. creation, 22
    of matter, 42–43
    of world, xi
artificial intelligence, 29
attention, 93

belief, vs. knowledge, 40–49
Bible
    and love, 87
    overview of, 85
    theology of, 83, 90–92
biology, 58
blessings, 98
bondage, and freedom, 18, 21

capacities, 25, 42, 61–62
captivity, 85
challenges, 23, 28
change, 45–46
chaos
    and corruption, 77
    and cosmos, xi, 42–43, 100
    and creation, 73
    and darkness, 39

    and evil, 16, 45
    formlessness of, 41
    and God's plan, ix
    vs. order, 18–19
    and purpose, 72
    and void, xi, 8, 21–23
children, of God, 97
civilization, 39
comfort, 98
communication, 10
compassion, 21
competition, 57–58
conflict, 15, 57, 61
confusion, and disorder, 24
conscience, 92
consequences, 35–36
consumerism, freedom from, 100
convictions, 40, 79, 82, 89
corruption
    and chaos, 77
    and death, 101
    death of, 38
    and destruction, 35, 61, 66
    ignorance of, 62
    opposition to, 59
    reality of, 17
    and religion, 86
    and violence, 10–11, 20–21, 23, 25, 31, 48, 54, 87
cosmos
    beginning of, 3
    and chaos, xi, 42–43, 100
    and matter, 103

INDEX

Could God Fall? The Fate of the Universe and the Faith of Christians (Wisnefske), ix
courage, 78–79
creation
    vs. annihilation, 22
    and chaos, 73
    and darkness, 26
    and destruction, 80
    and evolution, 83, 89
    goal of, 101
    and love, 8
    as solitary act, 84
    stewarding of, 62
    of the world, x
Creator
    as Destroyer, 1
    and the universe, 88
crucifixion, 86

damnation, deliverance from, 98
dark matter, 83
darkness
    and chaos, 16
    and creation, 26
    defiance of, 103
    deliverance from, 89
    and destruction, 31
    and happiness, 28
    vs. light, 15, 20–21
    opposition to, 24
    power of, 86–87
    reality of, 17–19, 22–23
    and sin, 25
    and void, 34
death, 29–30, 34–36
    and corruption, 101
deception, 45, 62
decisions, 55
deliverance, 84–85
    from chaos, 100
    from damnation, 98
    from darkness, 89
    and love, 7
desires, 55–56, 75
destiny, 24
destruction
    caring about, 26–40

    and corruption, 61, 66
    and creation, 80
    and hope, 68
    of life, 23
    and lifelessness, 88
    of universe, ix–x, 1–2
    and violence, 76–77
    of world, 15–26
devil, 45
dignity, 2–3, 8, 36, 54, 102
disinformation, 88
disintegration
    of matter, 42
    of the universe, 88
disorder
    and confusion, 24
    and energy, 25
    and life, 39
    vs. order, 7, 18–20, 44
    state of, 89
    and the universe, 26
doubts, 92
dreams, 75, 80–81
dualism, 17n1, 45
dust, 22

Earth
    future of, 38
    and heaven, 3, 27
    life on, 29
economics, 58
Egypt, 85
emotions, 3–4
energy
    chaotic state of, 62
    and disorder, 25
    and matter, 22, 33
    ordering of, 62
    and potential, 19–20
    and void, 100
Enlightenment, 9–10
environment, 5, 15
equity, 57
eternal life, 101
Eve, 35, 38, 39
evil
    and chaos, 16, 45
    and good, 31, 37, 39

knowledge of, 18
evolution
  of beings, 4
  and creation, 83, 89
  of life, xi
  of minds, 42
  of universe, 2, 43
ex vetere, x*n*1
existence
  beginning of, 84
  and love, 89
  and matter, 4
Exodus, 85
experiences, 36
extinction, 5

failures, 35–36, 87
faith
  acting on, 46–47
  exercise of, 94
  and hope, 6, 28, 90–91, 94–95
  and life, 99
Forde, Gerhard, 99
free will, x, 4, 71–79
freedom, 95–96
  and bondage, 18, 21
  to choose, 39
  and human beings, 23
  from slavery, 99–100
future, 80–81
  and the Earth, 38
  hope for, 40, 48
  of life, 32–34, 91
  needs for, 24
  for the universe, 22

Genesis, 85
goals, 79
God
  activity of, 45, 47
  children of, 97
  love of, x, xii, 18, 21–22, 91
  obedience to, 66
  as parent, 93
  plan of, 26
  power of, 48–49
  relationship with, 67–68, 94
  will of, 26–27

golden rule, 20–21, 31–32, 38, 53–55,
  58–60, 62–68, 90–91
good
  deeds, 99
  and evil, 31, 37, 39
  knowledge of, 18
gratitude, 32, 98–99

happiness, 1–3
  beliefs on, 23
  and darkness, 28
  pursuit of, 19, 30–31, 46, 53–57,
    66, 81
  vs. suffering, 48
harm, 21, 63–64
heaven
  and Earth, 2–3
  existence in, 34
  future life in, 23–24, 48
hedonistic paradox, 56
history, of universe, 84
hope
  and destruction, 34, 68
  and faith, 6, 28, 90–91, 94–95
  for future, 2, 40
  vs. knowledge, 9–11
  and love, 8, 19, 47–48
  for universe, x
  for world, 79–90, 100
humans
  as animals, 71
  enlightenment of, 20
  life of, 18
hypocrisy, 60

idolatry, 100
immortality, vs. mortality, 38
improvements, 36
inaction, 54, 77
inequities, 61, 64
information, vs. misinformation, 9–10,
  41, 44
insurrection, 102
intelligence, 3–4
interests, 27
Israel
  history of, 85
  people of, 100

Jesus Christ
  acceptance of, 21
  and law, 85
  life of, 8, 22, 86
John, 86, 101
judgment, 93–94
justice, 20

Kant, Immanuel, 9, 74
knowledge
  vs. belief, 40–49
  vs. hope, 9–11

laws, of the world, 19
Lewis, C.S., 17n1
lies, 45
life
  continuation of, 65
  and death, 36
  destruction of, 23, 88
  and disorder, 39
  evolution of, xi
  expenditure of, 87
  and faith, 99
  fragility of, 23
  futility of, 27
  future of, 28–29, 91
  of humans, 18
  of Jesus Christ, 86
  and morality, 54
  potential for, 42
  preservation of, 2, 57–61
  protection of, 43, 53, 84
  purpose of, x, 1, 49, 61–62
  reality of, 17
  sustainability of, 26
  threats and, 4
light, vs. darkness, 15, 20–21
love
  and the Bible, 87
  call to, 90–103
  and deliverance, 7
  effectiveness of, 9
  and existence, 89
  of God, x, xii, 8, 18, 21–22, 91
  and hope, 19, 47–48
  and matter, 25
  reality of, 17
  works of, 99–103
Luther, Martin, 93

macro view, 100
magic, 48
materialism, 43–44
  and free will, 72
  freedom from, 100
  and luck, 81
  and matter, 23, 41
  metaphysical, 61
  vs. theism, x–xii, 6, 16–17, 54, 74
  worldview of, 60
matter
  annihilation of, 42–43
  assumptions on, 82
  and cosmos, 103
  destiny of, 27
  disintegration of, 42
  and energy, 22, 33
  and existence, 4
  innate properties of, 16
  and love, 25
  and materialism, 23, 41
  ordering of, 62
  plan for, 42
  potential of, 24, 43
  scientists on, 40
  and void, 7
Mere Christianity (Lewis), 17n1
metaphysical view, 60
micro view, 100
militarism, freedom from, 100
miracles, 47, 85
misinformation, vs. information, 9–10, 41, 44
moderation, 56
morality, 5–6, 29–30, 32–33
  failings of, 92
  judgements of, 83
  law of, 20–21
  and life, 54
  principles of, 57, 59, 60, 73
  questions of, 55
  rules of, 62–68
  wisdom of, 10
mortality
  vs. immortality, 38

and morality, 30
motivation, 90–93
multiverse, 33
mutations, 10

natural forces, 7
natural laws, 33, 44–45, 94
natural world, knowledge of, 40
nature, 26–27, 40–41
nothingness, 1, 103

obedience, to God, 66
obligation, 72
opportunities, 73
optimism, 81
order
    vs. chaos, 18–20
    vs. disorder, 7, 44
origin, 41

panpsychism, 42
pantheism, 42
patterns, 46, 88
Paul, 26
peace, 48–49
Pharaoh, 85
plan
    of God, 26
    for matter, 42
platinum rule, 64
potential
    of energy, 19–20
    for life, 25
    of matter, 43
    of nature, 47
    of universe, ix, 89
power, of God, 48–49
prayer, 46
preservation, of life, 2
principles, 44, 87
prophecy, 33
protons, 15
purpose
    and chaos, 72
    lack of, 78
    of life, x, 49, 61–62
    of universe, 101

radiation, 19, 22
reality, 34, 42, 45, 49
reason, x
Red Sea, 85
regularities, 41, 44, 88
resistance, futility of, 54
resources, 28, 32, 57, 77–78
respect, 62, 64, 102
responsibilities, 30, 38–39, 46, 71–72
rest, 77–78
rules, 37, 39

salvation, 92
sciences, 60, 82
scientific method, 5, 9
security, 27, 59
self-awareness, 35
self-destruction, 4–5
self-interest, 23, 59
self-love, 59, 98–99
self-preservation, 4–5, 23, 38, 49, 55, 58–59, 61, 66, 76
self-sacrificing, 97
service, 96
servitude, 75
silver rule, 63–66
sin, 8, 25, 101
slavery, 74–75, 85, 101–2
solidarity, 28
souls, xii, 16, 56
standards, 37
stewards, of Earth, 23–24, 46
struggle, 59–60
success, 87
suffering
    vs. happiness, 48
    and theism, 81–82
survival, 57–58, 60

temptation, 29, 31, 37–38
theism
    and free will, 72
    vs. materialism, x–xii, 6, 16–17, 54, 74
    and suffering, 81–82
theology, of the Bible, 83, 88, 90–92
threats, 64
truth, 40

tyranny, 85

uniformities, 83
universe
    beginning of, xi
    and the Creator, 88
    destruction of, ix–x, 1–2
    development of, 19
    and disorder, 26
    future of, 22
    history of, 84
    and life, 103
    vs. multiverse, 2
    potential of, ix, 41, 89
    purpose of, 101

values, 36, 60
violence
    acceptance of, 35
    and corruption, 10–11, 20–21, 23, 25, 31, 48, 54, 87
    and destruction, 39, 76–77
void
    and chaos, xi, 8, 21–23
    and darkness, 34
    and energy, 100
    and love of God, xii
    and matter, 7
    opposition to, 89
    and the universe, 1
volition, 3–4

waste, 28
will, of God, 26–27
wisdom, 20, 42
wishes, 56, 80
Wisnefske, Ned, *Could God Fall? The Fate of the Universe and the Faith of Christians*, ix
works, of love, 99–103
world
    bettering of, 27, 47
    creation of, x
    destruction of, 15–26
    hope for, 79–90, 100
    laws of, 19
worldviews, 3–9, 29, 53–54, 61, 66, 79–80

www.ingramcontent.com/pod-product-compliance
Lightning Source LLC
Chambersburg PA
CBHW071219160426
43196CB00012B/2349